NE

WALKING in the SPIRIT

DR. SHARON MANCHA

ISBN: 978-1-80128-468-4

Dedication

A special thanks to my loving family and to God for the revelations and grace He provided to focus on this book after all of the events that were hindrances. You can imagine the spiritual warfare I faced in endeavoring to move forward in the third book for liberating and empowering the hungry ones for God who fight your way through the trials to the table of the Lord to feast in His presence.

Acknowledgment

I would like to thank my beautiful daughters, Khalilah and Abigail, who, with persistence, encouraged me to write and were instrumental in my completing this book on time as they value the wisdom and revelation that God has called me to share with the world. Their love and untiring support were an inspiration as God used them in this season as spiritual midwives in my birthing of this book to the world.

About the Author

Dr. Sharon Mancha has spent the majority of her adult life serving God and His people. Lady Mancha served as Co-pastor for twenty-seven plus years and now resides as Senior Pastor of Launch Church, COGIC in the city of Mesa, Az. Dr. Mancha has a deep passion for assisting believers in Jesus toward developing and maintaining an intimate relationship with God that leads to spiritual maturity. She has ministered and taught God's Word for many years, establishing hope in the hearts of many to pursue the open door of God to walk in the Spirit. She has authored two books, "The Power of Intimacy with Christ and Trial Trauma." Her dedication to the Body of Christ and hungry souls is that they may know God and discover an authentic relationship with Him that forces their spiritual IQ and produces within them a life filled with evidence of the presence of God actualizing in them the realness of His presence.

Contents

Dedication.....i
Acknowledgment.....ii
About the Author.....iii
Chapter 1: God Wants Relationship.....1
Chapter 2: Walking with God is a Journey.....13
Chapter 3: The Divine Manifestation of Love.....25
Chapter 4: The Heart Work.....36
Chapter 5: Bringing Self to God.....66
Chapter 6: Prayer and God's Promises.....85
Chapter 7: Discerning the Spirit of God.....92
Chapter 8: The Power of the Word of God.....102
Chapter 9: Next Steps.....106
Chapter 10: Illuminated by Walking in the Spirit.....113

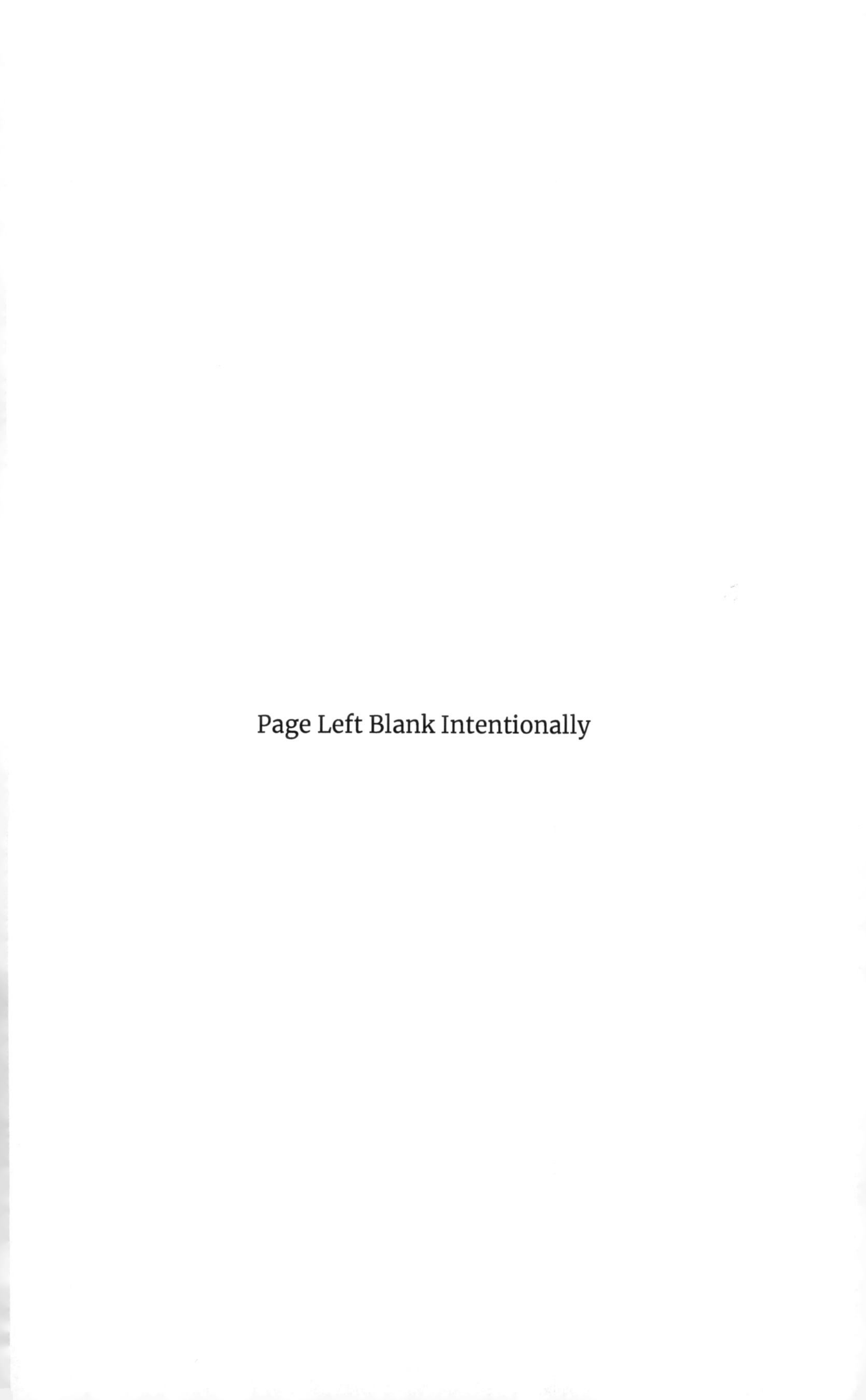

Page Left Blank Intentionally

Chapter 1: God Wants Relationship

God wants to have a relationship with each of us to bring us back to Him so that we might inherit the kingdom of heaven. Sadly, many people struggle in developing a relationship with Christ because they think He is abstract and at a distance from them or that he is not a personal savior. Since most of us were not trained from infancy to have a relationship with God, you will need to be intentional about practicing living from the heart. Many seekers try and serve God with their minds and leave out their hearts or from only their hearts and neglect their intellect. Some may suppress their emotions and try solely to use logic, but merging intellect and heart is the combination necessary to a life of faith that situates us in the power of God for refining our sensitivity to God's voice.

While you may have learned to access your heart as the only process for reaching God, it is also important to understand your mind is a key partner in ensuring you clearly understand God's will for your life and ministry. Not developing a disciplined focus on bringing your entire being to God will cheat you out of the revelations the Holy Spirit wants to share with you. In over two and a half decades of ministerial leadership, I have seen many people struggle to open their hearts and let God walk with them as Lord and life-guide. Choosing to live a fulfilled life through a relationship with God demands connectedness to Him and yielding to the courting of you by the Holy Spirit. It does not matter your ethnicity, financial status, or culture; some are challenged with letting God into their heart space because of some trauma or distrust that occurred in life, which makes them hesitant to form true intimacy with God because trusting anyone is too risky for them. The human experience and misshapen relationships sculpt us to protect our hearts and avoid hurt resulting in hiding the damage from God and keeping us stuck in an unhealthy emotional life. This type of behavior sections the heart off, leaving it to become a sacrosanct place where only a few people are granted access.

To form a relationship with Christ, we must come from the heart and come to him real and vulnerable. We must possess a desire to yield to God's presence if we are to experience the blessings He offers and grow our faith for walking in the Spirit. To receive him, we must hear his voice and answer, Rev. 3:20. To discern the workings of the Holy Spirit, the heart must be activated to the Holy Spirit and learn to be receptive to God's love.

So, I'll be talking about two very important things in this chapter: the first is to realize that God calls us to an intimate relationship with Him leading us into walking in the Spirit, and the second thing is how to yield to it for experiencing God in our daily lives. The journey starts with the heart and evolves and matures as your ability to recognize the voice of God for following his lead, right into the Spirit of God. This process matures your spiritual discernment, which is necessary to learn how to walk in the Spirit of God. Obeying God requires using our heads, accessing our hearts and embracing God's Word. The journey starts with the heart, so you must learn to open up and feel His love; you won't begin growing in God until you take this first step toward surrendering to Him through believing in scriptures, trusting God's voice, and walking out your faith. The wonderful thing is that Jesus already did most of the work.

God first initiates this connection to call us into intimacy with Him. This event can occur at any place and season in your life. It's those extraordinary circumstances that tend to shake a person to respond to God's love and call. God courts us and sets us up for our first encounter with him. He knocks at our heart's door.

"Here I am! I stand at the door and knock. If anyone hears my voice and opens the door, I will come in and eat with that person, and they with me." ***-Revelation 3:20***

As the verse says, one must hear and yield to God's solicitation to establish a relationship with Him. The person must be able to hear and recognize His call and must answer and yield by opening their heart to God, and keeping it open for Him to continue to reveal Himself. This is when we first meet Jesus Christ.

This meeting is not a singular affair, for the Lord will talk to us at different times in our journey. Your response to His call will determine your life-changing transformation into the kingdom of God. One can tenderize their heart to be more receptive through reading the Word of God, receiving the preached gospel of Jesus Christ, and igniting within them the powerful transformative power of prayer.

When you feel that warm love and presence of God, embrace it and allow the Holy Spirit to shower you with His love and peace. Just simply say yes and yield to Him. Don't allow times of fear and opposition to hinder you from accepting the love of God into your life as there is a revelation to be discovered and an opportunity to encounter the Spirit of God.

If you fear Him because He is invisible, ask Him to help you to trust Him enough to tell Him yes. Risk trusting God, and He will help you to yield your spirit to His. Ask Him to teach you how to do this, teach you how to respond to Him, respond to Him in a depth that will center your heart in the safety of His eternal love and care.

Instead of allowing fear of the unknown or the chatter of any opposing external matter, try to focus and keep your heart in that holy place, where God can reveal Himself to you in a way that that will secure your faith in Him and deepen your joy of His presence living inside of you. Embrace God's presence, be consistent in prayer and meditate on relationship with Him and His Word. Determine to overcome the distractions of the mind from the busyness of the day. It is important to increase your pursuit of Him, channeling the love of God in your soul to live authentically in His illumination because He is God, and you are His.

We must truly open our hearts to God and be vulnerable, for there is no chance He will betray us like others may have. Fight the temptation of fear and trust God, our creator, for He desires what is best for you. When I first experienced connection with God, I was overwhelmed with peace, and it felt so good. It was like my whole body and space were filled with love, joy, and peace. I felt energized like never before, and all I could do was weep in awe and prostrate myself before God. I never wanted the feeling to stop, but when I came out of the Spirit and realized I had encountered the supernatural, fear of the unknown tried to tempt me to not yield again, but I pressed past it right back into intimacy and overcame.

I knew God only wanted to bless me with His love. When God would visit me, there was the powerful presence of God comforting and securing my confidence in Him. It was so good I kept coming back for more. When fear would try and overtake me, and I retract some, He would lift from my presence, and I would feel cheated. I began to miss Him and called out in prayer, asking Him to return and help me defeat fear. I wanted to feel God and let go of any doubt or fear.

At the very beginning, the adversary of our soul was trying to hinder my connection with God through fear. My very first battle was to face it, fight, and overcome, and I did. Praise be to God! I wanted God to be active in my heart, and I fought my way through because I missed his presence. This was the first lesson I experienced, which taught me to want God enough to press against obstacles or hindrances spiritually and naturally. They say absence makes the heart grow fonder, and I realized from the first encounter with God that I wanted what He was offering, himself, and I wanted it bad enough to face fear and seek God in prayer for strength and courage. Then, the Lord answered my prayers and began to teach me how to remove the doubts in my head and yield my heart to him for healing, restoration, and empowerment. When I overcame, I cried my heart out in thanksgiving, for I knew the value of the blessing I had been given. I yielded, letting God come in like a flood, His warmth flowing through my heart, washing away the fear and blessing my soul. My soul longed for the love of God when he gave me the victory. I knew it was the Lord; there was no question in my mind that no other power could match this love and His holiness. It is a state that cannot be described in words. There is no experience more peaceful or more enticing than being born of the Spirit and finding intimacy with Christ.

It is why I write this book and work in ministry. The Lord told me to convey His message to you so that you, too, could experience his love and grace and for you and I to go tell the world. Don't get stuck in the past, letting fear prevent you from establishing a full relationship with God. When we walk with Christ, we learn to live an authentic and purposeful life. Once the connection is made, it will become your most precious treasure; no one can steal it from you. You have to surrender it, and so you must fight to keep it, don't yield it for anything or anyone.

The power that flows from the presence of the Holy Spirit makes you capable of enduring anything the world can throw at you. You will no longer be fooled by falsehood and will recognize the hand of God working in you and in the world around you. Relationship with Him allows you to become the best you. Your life is empowered, and you will develop a desire to learn more about God and His kingdom. The evangelism and prophetic work of God in me was revealed as I became intimate with God. You must be willing to trade in everything to maintain this relationship; nothing worldly should supersede your relationship with God. The enemy will try to steal this priceless treasure, and you have to fight tooth and nail to make sure you maintain it, and it is not sifted by the enemy's tricks to deceive you out of relationship with God. Nothing in the world can compare to the richness of living and working in God's kingdom. The output of relationship with God will pour out into your life, work and ministry.

However, you are a lot more effective when you learn to hear the voice of God and recognize His work, so you can move at His beck and call. You will need to be intentional and maintain commitment because the adversary will try and sever your relationship with God. The enemy will use every tactic to try and trick you away from God. Your life may become busy or chaotic, or distractions will try and keep you from communing with the Holy Spirit. Don't be nulled to sleep, stay focused, and do what is needed to nurture the call of God

The enemy does not want you to be sold out to God or fulfilling God's will. When you are liberated, you present the threat of helping other people escape their worldly prison, which is a big threat to the adversary. Your personal connection with God fuels your life. Anything that takes away from it, avoid it like the plague. When you walk with God, you can discern the mind of the Spirit and become privy to his will. When we live in an intimate relationship with God, all things are possible.

When you read the Word of God, He reveals the true nature of His work and how the Word applies to your life, the kingdom of God, and the kingdom of heaven. Our weapon is the Word of God, fortified by faith in God and is only actualized in the Spirit and not of the carnal domain. As you learn to open your heart and have these encounters with God, He will visit you more and more.

Intimacy with Christ is essential as this relationship is strengthened. The times of prayer then represent points where this relationship with God becomes even stronger and deeper. If you sin or make a mistake, simply repent for your mistakes, get up, dust yourself off and get back in the race, and your relationship will grow and grow, and you will discover the power of God living within. If you fall short of obedience to the Holy Spirit or the Word of God, no need to keep up pretenses; admit your shortcomings and ask the Lord to help you return to a state of obedience.

God knows you more than you know yourself, so there is no use in hiding. Live in the state of righteousness. If you adopt a sinful lifestyle, it will cheapen and kill your living in intimacy with Christ. Salvation and grace do not give us a free pass to live in sin. A true believer with an intimate relationship thinks and lives in line with God. It is crucial to be sincere when repenting, and that repentance should lead back into faith and obedience. The Bible says,

"Godly sorrow brings repentance that leads to salvation and

leaves no regret, but worldly sorrow brings death." – ***Corinthians 7:10***

Despite all the signs all around us, there are many in the modern world who do not believe in God or that do not serve him in spirit and in truth. As stated before, the heart has to be open to receive and recognize His solicitation to intimacy. A sincere heart is a key to a relationship with God. We cannot fool God. He is the Spirit of truth. The scripture tells us that with the heart, man believes in righteousness. So, your heart is essential in forming and maintaining a relationship with God.

The question then arises, why do we need the heart? Why can't we rely on the head to achieve this relationship? God is visible to our physical eye; we can only see Him through our spiritual eyes and senses. Just as our physical body possesses senses to perceive the world, so does our spirit. Our relationship with God must be grounded in Bible. You must connect with the Spirit of God by faith in his Son Jesus Christ in the work of the Holy Spirit. The Bible is full of passion about God's love toward us and His desire for us to love Him back and to know Him through the Spirit of God.

Jesus taught Nicodemus of the spiritual experience, one that transcends the physical world. In the same manner, you must learn to recognize the Spirit of God engaging you. One thing that we can reliably use to verify and discern it is God is through the Word, the witness God left of his Son revealed in Bible derived by the inspiration of the Holy Spirit. God's Word is truth, and God works through his Word. Center your confidence in your relationship with God according to what the Bible teaches is the witness of how God would manifest Himself in the lives of believers. We don't want our possibility to experience and know God to be forfeited because of a natural assumption but by Spirit revelation from the Holy Spirit. Believe the Word and use it as a guide for discerning God in your life. The only thing eternal is His Word, and thus, the only reliable means of learning the truth. Jesus is the Word of God made flesh, so we must follow His example if we are to remain biblically grounded. Everything we experience must be filtered through this lens. This is only possible when we have been born again. As Jesus answered;

*"Verily, verily, I say unto thee, Except a man be born again, he cannot see the kingdom of God." **–John 3:3***

*Without a shadow of a doubt, this clearly states that those who are not born again will not inherit the kingdom of heaven or have supernatural experiences with the Holy Spirit through spiritual sight. To establish a genuine connection, you must be born again. **–John 3:4-5***

The birth of the spirit refers to repenting from sin and accepting Jesus Christ as our Lord and Savior according to the Word of God. Then, one follows on to receive the baptism of the Holy Spirit. When we truly believe and absorb this, the Word enters our hearts, and we are born again of the spirit. We die to the flesh and rise in the spirit. We live for the eternal instead of the temporary world. Answering the door when God knocks and continuing to hear and respond causes spiritual growth and births within a proclivity to a relationship with Him.

Walking with and responding to God is spiritual. Nicodemus

struggled to understand this because he kept using his logical thinking, believing he was dealing with a natural phenomenon. The truth is, walking with God can only be understood in the spirit because it is spirit. As the sixth verse states, the flesh and the spirit are distinct. The physical birth and the spiritual birth significantly differ; the latter is even more significant and real than the former.

Our mistake is to let the physical natural world and our senses supersede the spiritual. Yet, when you form an intimate relationship with God, you realize the limitations of your natural existence and must deepen your ability to trust God to guide you, but if you keep responding to God, your relationship with Him will grow stronger as you walk with Him. When you cross that threshold, the spiritual senses will feel more real than anything you experience in the flesh. Walking with God is eternal. As your relationship grows, your spiritual senses will become sharper, being untouched by age, unlike your physical body.

That spiritual conversion also modified our natural bodies. Our ears are attuned to hearing the voice of God, and our eyes learn to see God in His works. Our understanding and thinking learn to receive the Word of God and understand His wisdom. We perceive and see like Him. We drink the Word to sustain the spirit like we consume water to nourish the body. The time we spend in intimacy with God after being born again feeds our souls. When we live in Him, we live in spirit and truth, biblically grounded, beyond the natural understanding. The Word of God helps us discern His voice from our own and that of the world.

This is why Bible is so important as reading and believing in it refines our spiritual mind. When you reflect on the Spirit of Christ, others will begin to notice a change within you. People will know that you have been God. They will seek you to help them reach the same state. As you grow and learn in your natural life, the same process applies to your spiritual growth and development. We must let God reign, guiding our life through His wisdom. We act as God desires and dislike what he dislikes. We become living Bibles, acting out the meaning in our daily lives in our thoughts and actions.

This is why we must base our reality on Bible; else, the adversary can get an advantage over you as the Word has power over that which is not truth or the spirit of the error. The fruits of the Spirit must manifest in every single aspect of life. Wherever there is a shortcoming, ask God to forgive you, and he will, and you will maintain a relationship with God. When living in a relationship with God, we learn to see our own heart, a true reflection that only the mirror of the Word can provide. You have to stay in rhythm with God, creating a balance that prevents you from going overboard in self or religion. We must always be open to learning, else we become stubborn and stuck, failing to fully realize our relationship with God as evolving and maturing. We also limit our ability to clearly see ourselves as God does, so we must continue to be transformed into the image of His Son, Jesus Christ. Like a growing child into maturity, we need the guidance God provides to mature our spirit. Use your heart as the altar, where you slay the flesh and anything that contradicts God living in you, and embrace the power of God that is released when we live in the Spirit.

Chapter 2: Walking with God is a Journey

I have been walking with the Lord for over 37 years, and it has been a blast. There have been highs and lows, adventures, and experiences with God that stretched me to spiritual maturity. There have been so many things that I've learned about myself, God, the kingdom of God as well as how the Christian community connects to God, the working of the Holy Spirit in the corporate anointing, and all of those elements that involve the spirit realm and the community of Christian fellowship.

I want to share with the Body of Christ across the globe how important it is to walk with the Lord in the Spirit. From creation, God has desired to walk in relationship with human beings as our God. He has spoken all things into existence and desires to speak into our lives, healing, and wholeness of heart, spirit, and mind. When we positively respond to His love, He provides the power to live the abundant life of biblical text and to be effective ministers of the gospel.

This is activated as we respond to God with a yielded heart and spirit. His expression of intimacy toward us is present everywhere, in the very creation of the earth and in our likeness to him. His passionate love for us is apparent in how we were created. That longing for a relationship with him abides deep within every soul but is only ignited when encountering him and responding with an open heart of acceptance. We are only truly satisfied when we surrender our hearts to Him for total healing. This encounter leads to whole-life success if we continue to respond to his love by obeying his voice and being led by the Holy Spirit into a life of joy and peace. It's crucial, as we talk about walking with God, that you reflect on where you are with the Lord. Jesus is the Word made flesh, and He came to live inside of us, so we must reflect from the heart on who we are in Him and who He is to us.

Jesus loves and cares for us and requires us to respond to His love through allowing the power of the Word of God to be rooted in our hearts, minds, and spirits, for Jesus is the Word of God. As said in John 1:1, *"In the beginning was the Word, and the Word was with God, and the Word was God."* We must live according to the scripture. I want to start off by talking about what it means to walk with God. Walking with God is putting your hands in the hands of the Lord, making an intentional effort to spend quality time with Him every day, getting some Bible time, even if it means turning on your Bible app and listening to the Word being read while driving, working, etc.

I'm not talking about a commentary or listening to preaching, I'm talking about the Bible itself, turning on a chapter and letting it be read to you while you're getting dressed in the morning, or you're sitting down and reading the Word of God. So, walking with God is getting to know God's Word, allowing it to get into your heart because He said that He would write his Word on the table of our hearts. In order for God to write His Word on the table of our hearts, we have to spend time with the Word of God, to allow the spirit of the Word to become entrenched in us and that our lives are lived out of the relevancy of the scripture every day. From an intimate relationship with Christ, we're able to gather nuggets of wisdom that empower us to empower others. So, a relationship with your Bible deepens your relationship with God. Working with God is important to your success as a believer and for your whole life's success. Whatever you want to do in God, whoever you want to become in God, whatever legacy that you want to leave, everything is connected to walking with God, and this is a lifetime journey. When you are in that rhythm of relationship with God that flows through your life every day, it will empower you to live, thrive, and become.

If you don't eat the Word of God and have a relationship on a daily basis, then how are you going to really get to know God? Because the Word of God and the Bible itself are God's revelation of Himself. It's God's revelation of how He feels about His church that He bought and purchased with His blood.

When you avoid developing a relationship with God and His Word, then you can't come to know who God is, what God wants, or expects from us as believers, how He wants to connect and have fellowship. It's important that we form this intimate relationship with the Word of God if we're going to walk with God because God doesn't work outside of His Word. He works through His Word because His Word is the revelation of Jesus Christ. It's impossible to say that "We know God, and we walk with God, but we don't have any authentic foundation of faith in the teachings of the Bible." We're not going to be stable or very spiritually strong. If Jesus is the Word of God made flesh, according to the scripture, and we know that He is, then you're supposed to build your life upon the Word of God. To have a relationship with God means you have to have a relationship with your Word. That's the initial part of walking with God – to be devoted in your pursuit to make Jesus the Lord and Savior of your life. You must put your hands in His, pick up your Bible, and begin to form a relationship with the Word of God. This will allow you to come to know the mind of Christ. You come to know Christ through the Word since He is the Word, made flesh, and dwelt among us. We must know the Word in order to know God.

It is always far better to know your Bible than it is to know Christian clichés, trends, and movements because they come and go like everything else; they get recycled over and over again. But when you know your Bible, you can be rock solid in the Word of God. You can then present that Word to God and expect answered prayer. There have been times in my life when I've had some difficult seasons.

Those were the times when I needed to hear from God. I needed to know what the Lord had for me and what He wanted me to do, so I could maximize my life in Him. But I had to say the Word of God, so the Lord would quote back to me the scripture that was inside of me. I would read, bring that Word up, and that Word would be the answer to whatever the situation was. That Word would be grounded by faith in God because without the Word of God, there isn't very sound faith.

We need our faith to be established on the Word of God because you can hold God to His Word, but you can't hold Him to trends and fables. You can hold Him to the Word of God because He is the Word and the Word is what He gave us, as our map to heaven, and as an instructional manual on how we ought to live as Christians and how we are to please God. It is the revelation of the will of God.

Practice What You Read

Next, I want to talk about how important it is for you to establish a relationship with the Word of God, that when you're reading your Bible, you're actually making the decision to live out what you read in the Word of God. As you walk with God, you can have an honest conversation with God, such as "Lord help me to live," "Help me to be an example of the fruits of the Spirit," "Help me to live a life that glorifies you." "As I walk with you, teach me your ways, open up the eyes of my understanding, show me where I come short in living your Word.

"Lord, please show me where I fall short." Say this so that you form a very conscious and intentional relationship with God that transform your behaviors, your attitudes, and your thinking system to ensure your thinking isn't stinking. Walking with God requires intentionality. Ask the Lord to give you the strength to sustain the change that you and He together make in your life. Walking with God is intentional.

Intimacy and Consistency in Prayers

We have to do the things that grow our faith in our relationship with God. You're perhaps just at the beginning or in the middle of the growth process, but you need more – we all do. It's important to have consistency and faithfulness to a church fellowship, gleaning in Bible study to get a deeper and greater understanding of the Word of God. You will receive revelation that's deeper than the one that you already have.

Hence, walking with God – attending Bible study, going to the church, having the quality time of prayer are all so very important and is a part of being intentional about your growth journey. Growth and serving God is all a part of the journey and enlighten our experience of growth. These simple truths help us to delight ourselves in the provision of fellowship and ministry through the Body of Christ.

The Bible said, "Delight yourself in the Lord, and He shall give you the desires of your heart." – Psalm 37:4. When we delight ourselves in God, we'll know that we're going to receive from Him all the things that we desire according to his will. Considering that, you should make time to delight God - that time of worship, prayer, or meditation - by which you just give God the praise for all the marvelous things that He's doing in your life. If you do that, you will find that your joy in Christ will accelerate. It will become real and authentic. Our strength in God will increase because Bible tells us that the "Joy of the Lord is our strength." – Nehemiah 8:10. The more we spend time acknowledging God, giving Him the glory, being grateful toward Him, praising Him for His activities in our lives, for the things that He reveals in our lives, will be the more God will manifest Himself in our life. Your praises provoke God in your life and enrich your journey.

As Bible says, *"God inhabits the praises of His people"–* ***Psalm 22:3 KJV***

The Body of Christ

You don't mature in God by simply going to church only. We have to have our own individual pursuit of God, driving us to the heart of God and causing us to sit in God's presence, leading us to hunger and thirst after righteousness; as He said, "Blessed are those who hunger and thirst after righteousness, for they shall be filled." – Mathew 5:6. If you want to be full of God and experience the anointing while you're walking with Him in your daily life, you need to be intentional.

Be honest and authentic with God. Give yourself to God. Don't deny Him. Give Him the praise. Have some time of worship. Be consistent and faithful to your local church, your Bible, study time, and your worship time. This is part of the journey; the lived out life in Christ day-by-day.

The power that is available in a relationship with Christ is accessed through an intentional response of spiritual hunger for God that leads to a deepened intimacy. When a believer desires to know God, the Lord creates opportunities to discover Him. This may happen through preaching, teaching, and an evangelistic encounter, or a simple whisper from God into the heart of the seeker. Rather new seeker or a person who attends church but really doesn't know God, the Holy Ghost provokes a relationship. Responding to the love of God demands of us an intentional love that drives us to Him, to know and believe in the Word of God, and to be led by the Holy Spirit in our daily lives. Newly saved or old hat, God will call us all to a sincerity that leads to an intimate relationship with Him. Listen to the voice of the Lord. He will tell you to pray for somebody, give more in the offering, or whisper a word in someone's ear.

If He asks you to pick someone up for church and give them a ride, do it as God sees your sacrifice and will reward you accordingly. Perhaps their car is broken down, and they may not have confided in you, for they might be too ashamed to ask for help. If the Lord tells you to give someone a call and see if they need a ride, then you call and ask away. I can't tell you how many times that has happened to me. I obeyed the Lord's voice and called them up only to find out that they indeed needed a ride. Turned out they were too embarrassed to ask for it.

We are called to accentuate His provision and love in telling others that God desires a relationship with them. It is impossible to have an intimate relationship with Him and not love others whom He loves. This provokes us to tell others about the love of God. God's enriching love deserves our intentional response of love, service, and study of how to better please the Lord in our lifestyle and in how we demonstrate our love to others. Such small acts of kindness also build a stronger bond in the faith community because we are to be in harmony with each other. By being available to God to meet the needs of the Body of Christ, we're making provision, assisting, uniting, and supporting people. That's why we must have a local church, so we can serve in ministry. Everyone's not going to be T.D. Jakes or Joyce Meyers, we need to serve God in our routine and daily life activities.

Therefore, we need to participate in local churches, communities, marketplaces where God can use us as the means to serve others. It's in your everyday walk with God that He wants to use you. In your regular routine, you can be a minister to others, glorify God, and be obedient to Him.

Walking with God requires obedience to whatever He has called you to do. It doesn't matter what it is - how big or small – it is. It is the act of obedience that God blesses. He has no greater blessing for that one on the platform than He does for the one kneeling in the church at the altar. The work of a soul is the most rewarding experience that you can ever have, i.e., to see someone accept Christ and grow in His love. In Christ, there's nothing like the refueling of the Holy Spirit.

Ministers can birth a soul, and by the Spirit of God, we can cause a soul to regain their faith, to be restored, and be reconnected to God or find the faith to get to the next stage in God. When you are an instrument in the hands of God to change someone's life for the better, you are most powerful. These people will remember you going forward. You will build a legacy because of your faithfulness to God. Walking with God is an act of love for Him. This form of love is passionate, driven, and has a goal in mind. The goal to know God and to live out of love for Him is all at the heart of a sincere seeker. In response to His love, God will be busy in the life of the sincere. We must be in agreement with God to provoke change in our love language so that we can truly benefit from the will of God actualized in our relationships, family, business, and community.

As we experience and yield to His love, He strengthens us to be more successful in all that we do. You become an effective, efficient, and intelligent witness, an instrument, a tool, and a resource in the hands of the Holy Spirit. God's love and activity in our lives is revealed as we learn to discern His voice.

As God deals with you and proves Himself real and relevant in your life, He reveals His Word and causes that Word in your life to be real and vibrant. It is significant to your success and satisfying to your soul. God's Word and your intimate relationship with God deepens your conviction in God. It causes us to want to walk more intimately and to pay attention to our lifestyle because we don't want anything to separate us from the love of God.

As you fall in love with God, you'll see God in ways you never have before. Walking with Him causes you to see yourself. As you see within, you'll find that you mean more to God than you ever imagined. You'll learn that God loves you with everlasting love and that He is a God that is faithful to His people in every season of life, especially when it seems like He's nowhere around and is unaware of your needs. God is ever-present! In actuality, God is there all the time. When things seem all wrong, they're really alright.

There's a difference that one day can make. If you can hold on through the night, Joy cometh in the morning because God uses the time to work His will, so you can't get in a hurry. When we're walking with God, we have to wait on the Lord; as the scripture says, wait,

*"But those who wait on the Lord shall renew their strength. They shall mount up with wings like eagles, they shall run and not be weary, they shall walk and not faint." **–Isaiah 40:31 NKJV.***

There will be times in your life when you pray, but it will feel like God is not answering your prayer. That's your waiting season. When it seems like you really need an answer right then and there, but you aren't getting one, God may not be answering your prayer right at that moment because He's trying your faith to see if you will hold onto Him when the going gets tough, when it feels as though He isn't going to answer. He stretches your capacity of patience, endurance, and commitment to increase your spiritual maturity. When trials and tribulations arise, God wants you to know that He is there.

Whatever situation we're in, when things blow up, and the bottom seems like it's fell out, realize that God is yet to walk with you. He will definitely save you. The issue is that He doesn't want us to serve Him solely out of a feeling. If you are looking to always have to feel God in order to believe God, that is baby faith. He wants us to believe in Him when we can't feel Him. He wants us to believe Him because He said He would never forsake us nor leave us. "I will never leave you nor forsake you" – Psalm 55:22.

He wants us to believe in Him because He assured us that He

would be with us. He wants us to have that salvation that doesn't necessarily need a feeling in order to be real. However, God's Word proclaims it's real, and that settles it. God is not a man that could lie. He is faithful, even during times when we may not be faithful to Him.

Chapter 3: The Divine Manifestation of Love

In the midst of difficult times, we mustn't forget that "God makes beauty from your Ashes" – Matt 19:26. Remember, He is gentle and loving, kind and compassionate. Believing in God's great power enables Him to carry your burden and fill your soul with rest. The Lord reveals Himself as we deepen our relationship with Him, and we are enhanced to gather wisdom for the journey. Trust in the Lord with all your heart. Submit to Him, and He will make your paths straight. So, as we encounter difficulty in life, we can remember the hand of God and the activity of God as our source of strength.

The first time I learned to find shelter in God was when my brother passed away. Though I was much older than him, we were quite close. I was an adult when he was born, so he was more like a son to me. He was still quite young when he was murdered. I found supernatural peace and comfort in God. It was with the help of the Spirit of God that I was able to walk forward in God in spite of the grief. God was my strength and took me through it. Recently, I lost my husband. I, once again, found the love and care of God to carry me through this most difficult season in life. It was the Lord's love, His wisdom, and

His personal care for me were so significant to my healing and restoration– and it still is. It's been a couple of years since my husband's passing away; I find comfort in God and His Word everyday. I found ultimate solace in God in this most challenging time. I want my readers to know how to rest in God and be in His arms in the midst of the storms of life, for many may not be aware of its power and strength to comfort. I want you to understand that you can find shelter in God in difficult seasons of your life. Distressing and challenging experiences can turn your life upside down, making your future seem bleak, unclear, and undefined, but God is absolutely faithful. When we run into God, we find what we need and more for surviving, as well as thriving.

Finding shelter in God is anything but complex. It works by going deep down inside of your heart and spending time with the Spirit of God because Jesus said, "I stand at the door and knock. If anyone hears my voice and opens the door, I will come in and eat with that person, and they with me." – Revelation 3:20. In another instance, Paul provokes us to allow Jesus to reside in our hearts, that "Christ may dwell in your hearts through faith." – Ephesians 3:17.

To commune with God is to go within like you do when you're contemplating your life, meditating, and quieting your spirit. Go into your heart's space and rest there. You can still move about and perform your everyday chores and duties, but your spirit – the real you – can go on the inside of your heart with God and walk with God through the day and find intimacy with Him. This happens when you focus your attention on the motions and motives of your heart and embrace God as ever-present not just when you pray but at all times. You stay calm and attentive in there, far away from all the stress, pain, worry, and confusion. Go in there, and nestle in God's embrace. Talk to Him out of the sincerity of your heart and discover God is always present. Talking to the Lord calm your nerves, reduces stress, and provides peace. We must teach our mind and spirit to rest and be calm, to quiet ourselves. Another process is to meditate on God's Word and not let the noise pull you out of that place of serenity. So, it is all about practice. The more you practice, the easier it all becomes.

When grief struck in my life, I delve deeper inside of myself, seeking my place where the Lord meets me. He's always there, waiting on us. God's blanket of comfort instantly befell me. If you don't learn or practice being with God from your heart, then you are more likely to have an abstract kind of relationship with Him. It's God's desire that mankind develops an intimate relationship with Him - a relationship founded upon deep passion, security, trust, understanding, and faith.

When the Lord talks with us in that safe place of our hearts, He comforts, rejuvenates, strengthens, and empowers us. Therefore, it's necessary for believers to learn how to find intimacy with Christ, the safe place in the Lord, and embrace it as your place of empowerment, and experience God's absolute love. It's such a precious, gratifying place by which the flow of life's issues are refined. As you nourish the relationship, your authentic self becomes one with God's will. The Lord's presence, His wisdom, and His love are fully embodied in you in this place.

Being intimate with God allows you to become wise in a way that flows out to others' in kindness and compassion. Relationship with your Lord isn't abstract. It's real! You radiate from what you receive, and people can feel when God's people are authentic. Our relationship with our Lord is based on authenticity and vulnerability, so we engage more or less in the same manner with what He loves. As believers in God, we are strengthened and empowered to rest in the love of God and have our place of comfort and sense of security in God.

The Bible says, "The name of the Lord is a strong tower; the righteous run to it and are safe." – Proverbs 18:10. When we seek God and find Him, we discover ourselves in His "strong tower." It's a safe and secure place far from devils or demons. It's a place where the pains, confusions, and ineptness of life all go away. It's a place where you're more than willing to expose your raw, authentic self in the presence of God and find healing, restoration, and answers to unanswered questions. However, when God does not provide you with answers, you're still able to find and resolve your queries because of His comforting care.

I repeat; it's absolutely necessary to find the secret place within your heart where God, you, and His fellowship dwells. You have the ultimate place of safety and security that you can run into in the most difficult seasons of life. When life gets tough, overwhelming, unbearable, gloomy, and you find yourself in the pit of despair, turn to that quiet zone within the Spirit of God and give it to God for transformation. When no one understands, He does. When no one listens, He does. When no one is there to love, care, support, and provide for you, He is there for you. He is always waiting to hear from you and will respond. God knows us intimately and completely, so He's willing to teach us about ourselves, how we must treat others, how we should engage with others, how we must share His love with others, and how we must cultivate our relationship with Him. In this special place, we experience the true love of God. We come to understand the glory of God. We strive to learn about intimacy with Jesus Christ and are empowered by it to live a fulfilled life in Christ. Intimacy with the Lord is inspiring for others. It becomes a drive and passion for others to long for, to seek, and for learning how to acquire for gaining the only true and pure love of God.

This place of refuge God has provided is more powerful than our problems. It is stronger than the burden you are shouldering at the moment. It is more resilient than the sorrow you may be experiencing because it is a supernatural love. He has full knowledge regarding how to comfort; he created it, he will replenish, console, advise, and cause you to rejoice again, to view life in expectations and anticipation of the glory of God. Our Lord partners with us in this secret place and allows this union to advance your life. He becomes your biggest ally, providing direction every step of the way.

Time doesn't stay still. You will experience a new chapter, a new horizon, a silver lining, the next step in God's love. Our Lord knows how to satisfy the soul and to educate and encourage our soul to move forward towards destiny. Have faith in God. Embracing God is to see His vision and wholesome love and care for each of us. A deliberate and intentional effort to know God yields high dividends to those who dare to believe through the dry places into the fruitful flowing rivers of God's love for washing away hard seasons that tempt us to surrender our faith. Hold on and trust God, he will bring you out of the shadows into the light.

Embrace the truth of the Scripture, "He is our God forever and ever, and He will guide believers into victory." – Psalm 48:14. God will walk with you no matter how thorny the road is. He will walk the hard walk with us, comforting us all along; because He loves us unconditionally. His love is perfect. When we fully experience His love, we have nothing to fear. We can envision God's love in that with Mary and Martha, who were crying uncontrollably over Lazarus's death. They were wailing and seeking Jesus Christ. They believed that had He been there, Lazarus would not have died. And that's true. There's a possibility that he had not died if Jesus Christ were present.

However, Jesus's absence at the time of Lazarus's death was neither abandonment nor was an inability to resolve the problem. The problem was that Mary and Martha didn't understand the power of resurrection. They failed to comprehend that Jesus was the resurrection and that Jesus was not limited.

Nothing is impossible for Jesus Christ. He can go into our past and heal. He can turn our yesterdays into an abundant expression of His love for our tomorrow. Just as Jesus cared about Mary and Martha and loved Lazarus.

Jesus being the resurrection, he had the utmost power to speak to Lazarus and bring him forth and to give him a second chance at life and more time to spend with Jesus Christ and his loved ones. The powerful expression of God's response to Mary and Martha's grief is a manifestation for you and me today. Know that He has all the power in this world and beyond to heal.

He has the power to change our lives in the blink of an eye. He has the power to bring about a prosperous situation out of poverty, natural or spiritually. It's never too late for God to heal, restore, and resurrect things. Though He may not resurrect the loved ones you have lost, remember in your heart that He can resurrect us from the place of pain. He can raise you out of your ashes and bring you into a place where you are able to excel in God and thrive again.

He's the ability to help us live past the pain and sorrow because He is a healer. He is a God that is most compassionate and merciful. When called upon Him, He does interfere and get involved with the affairs of man. He's not only concerned about us being transformed by salvation, but He's concerned about our whole lives and our well-being. He protects us and looks after our physical, emotional, mental, and spiritual health.

God calls us to a sound understanding of the Bible. When turbulent times strike, we must remember the promises of Biblical texts. We can lean on God's word and have a solid foundation of faith that causes us to believe that Jesus is ever-present. We can extract the Word of God and implant it into our situations, so it can produce healing and clarity of thought and understanding. The realization that He is a loving God, a living

Savior, and that He wants to walk hand in hand with us. As a matter of fact, Jesus said, that "He has us in the hollow of His hand, and it is not possible for the devil in hell to pluck us out." – Isaiah 51: 16. By "the hollow of His hand," it means that Christ has us protected in a place of safety by His power.

As we read the Bible, we learn that the Scripture is a living Word. It is a tried-and-proven word. It is the manifestation of Jesus Christ, where Jesus is the Word made flesh. When we truly embrace the power of Scripture and witness that God left of Himself in the Biblical text, we're able to have a life of expected victory. By the Word, we're able to see Christ through the lenses of the revelation of God to us about His Son and the Holy Spirit.

We must not have a mystical ideal about God but a biblical one so we can apply it to our everyday lives and expect God to be a part of our human experience. We see it all through the Old Testament, the people of Israel experienced many challenging seasons and requested the power of God. They needed provision from God so they could move forward in their obedience and love for God. Even in times when they were disobedient, they cried out to God, and He responded to their pain and discomfort. He brought ease to their challenges. He's the same God as the Bible says, "and is the same yesterday, today, and forever!" – Hebrews 13:8. He loves us, and He won't forsake us, as His people individually and as the church - the body of Christ. The Word gives evidence of the handiwork of God, the life of the church. As baptized believers, we are positioned in Christ and in the Kingdom of God and discover access to His resources. God made plain to Israel through his dramatic intervention in Israel and our affairs, proved his love for his people. His care and affection never ceased. "Indeed, heaven and the highest heavens belong to the Lord your God; also the earth with all that is in it."

The Lord's infinite and everlasting love and grace renew every day; his unconditional favor and love for us are alive today and forever. It's available to you and me every day. All we have to do is tap into it and get in touch with God. Find hope and supply in your demanding seasons of life. In these seasons, God manifests Himself.

God shares with us in the Old Testament His passion for His people and how He will defend them against their enemy, and He created a place of worship in the tabernacle; so that they could visit in a designated place and they could have a heart-to-heart with Him. Where they could exercise their love and faith toward Him, and then, in return, He would exercise His love, provision and care for them. However, in the New Testament, it's done in our hearts which is our place of worship. Our bodies become the place by which we fellowship with God, seeking, developing, and responding to God's engagement - his solicitation for relationship. So, in the New Testament, we learn how to go deep within, where the Lord dwells after we have given him access to our hearts, and hear His voice. Again, God said, "I stand at the door and knock; If any man hear my voice, and open to me, I will come into him and my father, and we will fellowship with Him, and He with us." – Revelation 3:20.

It's clear that inside of our hearts, we have the ability to hear God. God speaks to us in our hearts, and we are empowered to hear God's voice. It is a discipline. It is paying attention to God's voice. He said, "My sheep hear my voice, and I know them, and they follow me: and I give unto them eternal life, and they shall never perish, neither shall any man pluck them out of my hand." – John 10: 27 – 28.

Open your heart to God that He may continue to speak to you and develop your hearing. In agonizing seasons of life, find God within. He ministers to us as we receive God in our inner self that we may evolve and reflect the presence of God and spread the aroma of our engagement with God to the world.

It is impossible to go into God, into that spiritual shelter, the refuge, or that place of intimacy, and not be transformed by the presence of God. It is life-changing in every sense of the word. It's a beautiful light that transforms everything from your heart to your spirit to your overall well-being. This place of healing where we find God is also where the rivers of life are flowing through our continued nurturing between God and us. It is a place where we learn how to engage and accept God. It is the place by which we come to know how God works within us and where we fine-tune our discernment of God's voice. Once you begin to spend time with God in the secret place - inside your heart – God will speak to you. The closer you move in, the deeper you connect with God. You will be able to recognize His voice and identify Him, and thereby learn how to follow the lead of the Holy Spirit. When we embrace this relationship and accept God's glory over us, seek to obey His voice, and follow His example, our lives are transformed.

Accept God and allow Him to be dominant in your life. This is when Jesus becomes Lord of our lives. The Bible plainly teaches, "Commit your way to the Lord; trust in Him, and He will act." – Psalm 37:4 – 5. Allow the Lord to be Your Lord. He will be your guide. So, it's important for each of us to allow God to be the Lord of our lives. He heals us out of painful places into places of joy. He exposes us and births within us godly wisdom, understanding, and spiritual maturity.

Being in this healthy place allows us to grow and find stability. Yes, you can be fortified and strengthened in the wisdom of God and the Word of God for life-empowerment. We develop confidence in His presence. Hence, we must find that secret place of the highest. It is the place where you can find resources for happy living. It's a place worth searching for. It has the supply needed to survive the journey we call life.

"Your unfailing love, O LORD, is as vast as the heavens; your faithfulness reaches beyond the clouds. Your righteousness is like the mighty mountains, Your justice like the ocean depths. You care for people and animals alike, O LORD. How precious is Your unfailing love, O God! All humanity finds shelter in the shadow of Your wings." - Psalm 36:5-7

I hope that everything I have shared so far gives you the strength and resources to be able to find that place in your life sooner than ever.

Chapter 4: The Heart Work

We are called of God and are called to live in expectation of the abundant life that Christ promised in the scripture, it is so essential to our joy and happiness. It is necessary that you tap into God's call to your individual heart work. It is a part of your privilege to experience the abundant life fueled by the resources of God. And to pull into your reality, the authority of God. The power of the scripture is to increase your confidence in God's love as you do the necessary heart work for spiritual maturity.

So, in this chapter, we will focus on heart work, what it means is to grow our hearts for dispensing from it our spiritual life resource that has the powerful influence of God to change our life, family, and community. We must focus on how to live out of the power of intimacy with Christ. Once we learn how to live out of this place, we become spiritual dispensers of God's love, empowerment, and are gifts to our world.

Remember, the Lord is not a partial God. He is not a God that loves one over the other. He's not a racist God or a preferential God where He prefers the rich or influential. He's not a classist or chooses the wealthy over the poor. He's not a cliquish God, where He appreciates a particular social group over another or one person over the other. He's not a fashionable God, where

He's not concerned about what you look like in your outer appearance. He's a God of the heart and spirit and solicits truth from us in our inner parts.

Psalm 51:5-7 KJV

[5] Behold, I was shapen in iniquity; and in sin did my mother conceive me. [6] Behold, thou desirest truth in the inward parts: and in the hidden part thou shalt make me to know wisdom. [7] Purge me with hyssop, and I shall be clean: wash me, and I shall be whiter than snow.

He's a God that cares about how you are overcoming in life and if your heart is pure and whole. It is important in reflection of God's love that provokes spiritual growth that we seek to know how to be spiritual dispensers of the transformed character we have experienced and grew, allowing others to benefit from this change. What are the things that flow from your heart into your relationships?

Proverbs 4:23

"Keep thy heart with all diligence; for out of it *are* the issues of life."

It is important that you do heart reflection; that you look on the inside and verify if you have that sweet, sincere relationship with God that is the center of your joy. Evaluate if you are actively engaged in your heart work as it is an artistry to refining your relationship with God. It is essential to be a student of yours and pay attention to what flows from your heart when in conversation and interaction with others and in a relationship with God. Be intentional about being a guard over your heart to make sure that it is being shaped after the counsel of the living God and is a reflection of God's Word, His Son, Jesus Christ.

The Lord loves you with an everlasting love, and He wants us to love ourselves. He wants us, through the relationship that we have with Him, to find his ultimate joy that strengthens and empowers us to be enthusiastic and excited about our journey walking in the Spirit. This motivation is most powerful when it is shared with our world. He works in both directions, heals you within and others and you are intentionally exposed to that transformative love of God that lives within.

God loves everyone. He never has to post a disclaimer that He loves, regardless of race, color, creed, religion, or sexuality. He is a God that loves every human being. He desires that we would come to Him and embrace his love for empowering our lives and those we encounter. This is part of that heart work we must do as believers so that we are made whole through the flow of God's love living within. This powerful union of our heart and God's love is contagious.

It will transform, empower and ignite the flow of God's love into our lives by which our souls are satisfied in Him, and our spirits are set on fire for God. Commitment to do the necessary heart-work is a decision to actualize your full potential naturally and spiritually and to live the life that God has made available to you. Heart work is an intentional discipline by which we walk with God on a daily basis. Proficient heart work requires that we discipline ourselves for the task of becoming sincere and a consistent commitment to self, and the Holy Spirit for developing the courage to face what you may discover about yourself and a willingness to do the work of change.

It is an intentional but focused endeavor. A lot of people never mature to the place of heart investigation or grow to the point of doing the heart work that leads to spiritual maturity for keener spiritual insight and a deepened sensitivity to the Holy Spirit. Hearing the Holy Spirit demands of us a yielded life and a refined ear, and that is matured to discern his voice as well as between good and evil.

Romans 8:6-8

6 For to be carnally minded is death; but to be

spiritually minded is life and peace.

7 Because the carnal mind is enmity against God: for

it is not subject to the law of God, neither indeed can

be. 8 So then they that are in the flesh cannot please

God.

A carnal mind is defined as: pertaining to or characterized by the flesh or the body, its passions and appetites; sensual: *carnal pleasures.*

not spiritual; merely human; temporal; worldly:

carnal[1]

It is essential to understand that it takes intentionality, discipline, honesty, and courage to look into your heart and to

[1] "Carnal Definition & Meaning." *Dictionary.com*, Dictionary.com, www.dictionary.com/browse/carnal.

be conscientious about doing the work for making sure that your heart is full of the spiritual fruit of God, the world resources that are to flow out of you into your world. Desiring to become all that is possible in God is also intentional, a decision to put your spiritual life upfront in how you value life is revealed when you commit to doing the heart work for partnering with God. Doing so is an on-purpose life decision that is rich with revealed truths about you and God's will, love, and commitment to your life success, as well as those powerful and invigorating life experiences in the journey that just simply makes it all worth the discipline.

Go for it, it is yours for the taking! Yes, you are provided for by God, but it is a daily journey. You can live the abundant life made available through Christ's work on the cross. The Bible said He despised the shame of the cross, but He endured it for the joy that was set before Him. I'm talking about the fact that Jesus went on the cross, got up out of the grave, justified believers in the Father, and then positioned us in Him so that we would be able to tap into what Jesus made possible for us.

Hebrews 12:2

2 Looking unto Jesus the author and finisher of our faith; who for the joy that was set before him endured the cross, despising the shame, and is set down at the right hand of the throne of God.

There is a heavenly warehouse of God, full of spiritual resources to make the abundant life that Jesus Christ promised available to those that believe in God. However, our partnership, spiritual discipline, and commitment are foundational to accessing and opening the door of the warehouse. Your authentic love response to God is the key to this privilege. God's love and your courage position you to unlock the riches of God. If you go after it with all your heart you will discover God's abundant love, grace, and mercy working with and in you to lead you into his provision and life supply personalized to you for your individual growth.

As you're walking through this journey, be intentional about your heart work and pay attention to your thoughts and emotions and sift them all through God's Word and keenly listen for God's leading so you make choices that grow you and deepen you. Focus on your responses as well, and then make conscious decisions – about the next steps and where they lead. Be very intentional about knowing the outcome so you don't subtract from your spiritual growth or hinder your relationship with God. Evaluate whether your feelings, thoughts, and behaviors are aligned with the things that are going to bring love to your life and enrich your ability to know and love God more.

Ask yourself, are my thoughts and emotions aligned with the Word of God? Are they in agreement with the wisdom of God, and then it is important to listen for and accept the answer? Be aware that it may not always result in what you want to hear or believe about yourself. It is important to be courageous and trust God when he does the deep revelation in you so that you may partner with Him for your heart work and make change for the good. Doing this work always leads to spiritual growth and empowerment within to become more proficient at spiritual discernment. When we reject what we see, we cheapen our growth and must repeat at some season the spiritual course again.

Remember, prayer is so key to developing the courage to do the heart work needed such as asking the Lord to give you the wisdom and strength to respond, behave, to love like He loves, and to be honest with yourself enough to evaluate and engage in the moments for maximum growth. Fight through the flesh to receive the power of intimacy with Christ for achieving spiritual goals and growth. It only happens if you want it and fight for it.

Our feelings, responses, and behaviors must glorify God in a way that yields a return to your life. This will increase your confidence and bring ultimate satisfaction to your soul. There's nothing like knowing that you please God.

Enoch had that testimony according to scripture that he pleased God, we can know that we please God, and we can reap the benefits of pleasing God. I understand that grace is there. I understand that salvation doesn't come by works. But Paul says, "You have faith, and I have deeds. Show me your faith without deeds, and I will show you my faith by my deeds." –

James 2:18

18 Yea, a man may say, Thou hast faith, and I have works: shew me thy faith without thy works, and I will shew thee my faith by my works.

There is the conversion experience by which we are to

manifest fruits of the spirit that are developed as we grow and walk with God. As we pay attention to who we are, how we behave, what triggers us, what makes us tick, what gives us joy, what causes us discomfort and look at these things with an intentional eye for evaluating and measuring them against the Word of God, then and only then are we able to discern if our lifestyle really glorifies God. If you discover that your lifestyle comes short of the biblical will of God, then do the heart work of change. The Holy Spirit is our companion and helps us to grow. He works on the mind and heart to promote our personal growth toward the things of God and our total conversion in mind, body, and spirit.

Romans 12:2

[2] And be not conformed to this world: but be ye transformed by the renewing of your mind, that ye may prove what is that good, and acceptable, and perfect, will of God.

The most wonderful thing about walking with God is that the Holy Spirit is there to teach us. He's there to help us, strengthen us, and give us the courage that we need to face whatever we need to face within ourselves; so that we can become our greater person in Christ Jesus, and God uses this transformation to reveal to the world the love of God and the power and authority of God that lives on the inside of us. It is a demonstration of your gratitude and thanksgiving to God for the work of salvation on the cross that should provoke your drive to heart work.

A life that has been transformed and is conveyed in conversion develops intimacy with Christ, which empowers our behavior and elevates our desire to be like Christ, the very image of Christ. When the world looks at us, they are to see the reflection of Jesus. The scripture states,

2 Corinthians 3:2-3

2 Ye are our epistle written in our hearts, known and read of
all men: 3 Forasmuch as ye are manifestly declared to be the
epistle of Christ ministered by us, written not with ink, but with the Spirit of the living God; not in tables of stone, but in fleshy tables of the heart.

When others look at our heart work revealed in our lives and observe our spiritual composure, they're able to see the love of Christ and the resources of God that have empowered our lives. It all is accentuated because of the way we respond, the way we live, the way we love life and express that love for God, ourselves, and others. For this to be the reality of your life, you must be intentional about the issues that flow from your heart. We must be intentional about the expressions of life that we express in our daily lives, how they fare, how they feel and appear to others.

Don't allow a hypocritical lifestyle by being one way at home and another in the church or in the community. Your heart should possess an intimate relationship with Christ. This relationship should empower your behavior, your words, and your authority over yourself. As a result, the expression of our intimacy with God flows out of our hearts into our lives and world. In other words, it flows into our existence. This heart flow causes us to be empowered by God to positively affect our families and communities. To have a word or expression and a witness in testimony is so powerful because we are in God, and any time we spend quality and intimate time with God, our lives are a power source for everything and everyone we touch and share with. We are called to be spiritual transformers, but the starting place is in the heart. So, to do this heart work, our intellect is required because walking with God is as much a mental thing as it is spiritual, for the warfare between flesh and spirit happens in mind.

Our thought processes are to be formed and molded in a way that reflects the authority and the power of the Word of God in our lives. Why? Because the Word of God is power. It is the believer's weapon of war. Understanding that we serve God with all the three parts of our being: the mind, body, and spirit and is crucial to do the heart work necessary to become and remain spiritually mature.

The resources of God become even more available as we grow in Christ. And as we yield ourselves to God, the Lord gives, empowers, and strengthens us. Generally, many people are living outside of their heart and spirit, never paying attention to what's within until something major happens and challenges them to the values of the heart. When there is a deficiency, whatever is inside of you erupts and comes out, poisoning the environment, ruining relationships, or hindering your witness as a believer. Do the heart work to become your best personhood in Christ. You have the power and authority in Christ to know what's in your heart, to be able to do the heart work that is necessary to mature into who God designed you to become. This process will equip you to get acquainted with the real you on the inside, the one God knows and loves. The one that responds and behaves according to what has been nurtured in the heart: good, bad, or ugly surfaces when the heart is provoked to respond during our most challenging moments. It will also manifest in the very pain of your reality or any situation that may have developed in you bitterness that is producing moments of behavior that does not glorify God and is revealed so you can change. Do the work of heart and be transformed to the glory of God.

Get in touch with your spirit, and live, thrive, and become. In the difficult moments of your life, when you feel negative on the inside, capture that emotion and speak the Word of God to it, do the work for your better. This is heart work. Heart work is the act of being accountable to yourself and to monitor what lives within your heart and spirit and to intentionally do the work of change from the inside out. This is possible through a relationship with Jesus. By deciding to partner with God for more spiritual control of your life issues, you will gain the power to capture and change any negativity in your life.

It is an act of faith! Use your faith in God to do the heart work. Indulging in the change work will help you bask in the joy of the Lord's glory. Speak the Word to your spirit and gird up the loins of your mind, meaning pay attention to your thoughts. Understand that some thoughts come from the devil. Don't assume all thoughts are yours. Some thoughts come from weariness when you're tired and fatigued. Some thoughts come from what you observe on the television or from daily experiences or conversations that you have with people. They manifest themselves later into thoughts and behaviors. These thoughts give rise to negative emotions – worry, anger, confusion, agony, etc., but you have to desire to do change work, and it begins in the heart and in your mind. Use biblical examples for understanding necessary steps and be tenacious to be courageous and committed to achieving them. God is your strength and sure success. When you roll up your sleeves and do your intention work of growth, the Holy Spirit will help you identify and understand your thoughts and emotions and how to take control of yourself and transform them. With intentionality, we make decisions to transform them into positive thoughts of love and joy, resulting in positive behaviors of love that birth change in attitude and healthy emotions. The Lord is our resource, and He has the power to overcome and transform all things. Trust him in you and trust yourself in partnership with Him. You have three-fold protection in God: God the Father, God the Son, and God the Holy Ghost working in your favor for your success as you yield and obey his lead.

Luke 10:19

19 Behold, I give unto you power to tread on serpents and scorpions, and overall the power of the enemy: and nothing shall by any means hurt you.

God has given us power and authority in Christ. He's empowered you to have the victory over every negative thought and emotion. Do the heart work, so you can be in control and in the stewardship of what comes in and goes out of your heart. It is necessary to live in the love of God and the authority of God, to transform the impulses and attitude so that the things that flow out of you glorify God and give satisfaction to your life.

Relationship with God is on the inside, in our hearts, mind, and spirit. Begin the confession work and proclamation of authority that Jesus has given you, and close that conversation in Jesus's name. You can perform all tasks with the name of Jesus. Jesus has invited, urged, and commanded us to pray in His name and has promised incredible results.

Everything we do and say should be done in His name (Col. 3:17). Over and over again in scripture, we read, "In my name," "In Jesus' name," or "In His name." The devils were powerless because of His name (Luke 10:17). The demons were cast out in His name (Mark 16:17-18). Healing occurred in His name (Acts 3:6, 3:16, 4:10). Salvation comes in His name (Acts 4:12, Rom. 10:13).

Regardless of where you are in your life with God, you can do the heart work essential to becoming of full age. Chase after God and pursue the love of God. The work that He did on the cross was sufficient. It was enough that you and I may have the joy that was promised to us by our savior, and this joy is accessed through the relationship with Christ and an intentional decision to walk and work in partnership with God for total life healing, restoration, and transformation. We can have the resources that were promised to us by Christ Jesus. He did the work, and His work was more than enough. The issue is we must have the courage, tenacity, and discipline to go after what God has made available. It is not an osmosis situation, that by just going to church, you're going to access the things of God. Rather, it is an intentional effort to embrace and pursue the things of God. It's a heart thang!

According to the Word of God, "It is clear that you are a letter from Christ to the world in the result of your ministry, written not with ink, but with the Spirit of the living God, not on tablets of stone but on tablets of human hearts." –

2 Corinthians 3:3.

I actualize and activate the word that has been written on my heart. I do so by proclaiming it, accepting it, and living it, and then speaking that word of God to anything and everything that comes against the word that has been written in my heart.

We cultivate that word seeded in the heart through prayer, Bible study, and listening to the preaching of the gospel and teaching from the 5-fold ministry, as well as quality time spent with God. As a believer, it's essential that you speak the Word to the circumstances and situations that try to plant themselves in your heart to derail your confidence in God, to impede your joy in the Lord, and to hinder you from being strong in the Lord. Dispense of it by rebuking it and not giving it place. You have been given the power!

Tap into God's love and begin your heart work. Tell the Lord that you love Him. Tell the Lord that you need Him. Tell Him that you want Him more than life itself. Begin your love language with God. Then confess and embrace the reality of God's love towards you. Convey your honest love to God. It is important that as you do heart work, you actually pursue the love of Christ and that you learn how to accept the love of God.

Activate it in your life by embracing and pursuing the love of God.

The Holy Spirit teaches us how to love God back in the God-enriched spiritual way. God loves each of us, and we must love Him back. Tap into the warehouse of God, or the resources of God, to actualize the love flow of God in and out of your heart. The power of love gives peace in difficult times. To ensure that the love of God is flowing through you and into our world, you must spend quality time with God and get to know His love. Express your love back to God, for we have to learn how to love God back. We don't naturally know how to love God, the Holy Spirit has to teach us.

In learning how to love God, peek inside of your heart. Be honest about what you see, hear, and feel. Measure it up against the Word and ask God to help you transform from within. Become intentional in your life, and transform those things that need to be changed through the help of the Holy Spirit. Live the Word of God. Embrace the power and authority of God, and it will strengthen you.

Thank the Lord through the process in your heart work with acceptance as God makes the transformation in partnership with your will and your effort toward God. As He helps you transform your behaviors, thoughts, and attitudes that might not please Him, know that God loves you. Demonstrate your love back toward God, the body of Christ, and the world around you, as Jesus died for you and it. God wants you and I to do heart work, so as life and attitudes of others impede and beat up on our lives and challenge our love because of our relationship with

Him, we're able to release the love flow of God and not respond in the flesh or with behaviors within us that do not glorify God.

How to Find Comfort in Difficult Times

When dealing with the matters of heart, you may feel like straying a bit from your work path because it can become intense but stay on track. He sees your difficulty, any trauma, and losses, fear and tragedy that may be going on in your world. We are to trust in the true and living God who cares about us, who loves us, and who has a plan for our lives. I want you to take away from this chapter that Jesus is a shelter.

He's a refuge. He's a strong tower which offers comforter in the Holy Spirit, and when we open up to be comforted. Lastly, understand that there are some things that you can do, personally and individually, to fuel your life. To be able to find that comfort in God, you can teach your spirit how to rest in God in hard times.

Remember, Jesus said, "And I will pray the Father, and He shall give you another Comforter that may abide with you forever." – John 14:16. And that's how we know that Jesus intended for the church – the people of God – to be comforted in the Holy Ghost and that we would find our full assurance, place of rest, and peace in the Comforter, the Holy Spirit. He walks alongside us in life and strengthens through our journey, gives hope in hopeless times, and brings scriptures to our mind that we may lean on God's Word. Lean into the Word and find shelter and confidence to face the difficult moments in life. God's provision is enough for your spirit and your soul regardless of the emotional stress felt.

The Lord knew that we would need Him. He knew that we would need a comforter. He was on Earth 33 years before he ascended on high. He knows the difficulty of the journey of the human experience.

The Word of Jesus, states "Unless I go away, the Advocate will not come to you; but if I go, I will send Him to you." – John 16: 7 – 8. While Jesus Christ walked on Earth, He was the comforter. However, then He added that I will send you another comforter, who will be with you always. He shall teach you whatsoever I have preached. He went on to say in another passage, "To preach my gospel by the Spirit, even the Comforter which was sent forth to teach the truth."

As we think about this comforter, He is a resource for living and surviving; finding the spiritual fortitude and the strength of God, to thrive spiritually, to be established in the truth, and to find hope in hopeless times. There is a peace that only God can provide. He said,

"And the peace of God, which surpasses all understanding, will guard your hearts and your minds in Christ Jesus." – Philippians 4:7.

He will give you the kind of peace, in the comforting of the Holy Spirit that will blow the minds of other people; not to mention that it will blow your mind first when you can run and find shelter in the refuge of the Lord, for the Lord is a pavilion and when the righteous run into Him, they are safe. We can find that the presence of the Holy Spirit leads and guides us into all truth, revealing the presence of God, His resources, and the power of the Scriptures for conquering all things.

As we read our Bible, the Holy Ghost brings the scripture to our hearts and minds. If we read that scripture and meditate on it, the Holy Spirit infuses it; because the Word of God is spirit. It's power. It's the Spirit of Christ, that is, Jesus Christ was the word of God made flesh. When we think about Jesus Christ, as the Word of God made flesh, the power of the resurrected Lord, and the authority of the Son of God, in Jesus Christ as the Son of God, we have confidence that in difficult times, we have the power to be able to live and to thrive in Him. He overcame the grave. He took away its victory and sting. He said,

"I have told you these things so that in me you may have peace. In the world, you will have tribulation. But take courage; I have overcome the world!" – John 16:33.

When we think about this awesome Lord and Savior, Jesus Christ, the gift, the promise of the Father that was poured out upon the Earth and was prophesied by Joel, this comforter the Holy Spirit, that would come and live in us, live through us, and then walk in companionship with us, that we might fulfill the will of God, and that we would have the power of the resurrected Lord, living inside of us, giving us the strength to overcome our troubles and obstacles and find the supernatural provision to take us through the storm. Now, what is the discipline of leaning onto the Lord? It is to have a devotional life, pursue a relationship with him, to seek after Him. He said, "You will seek Me and find Me when you search for Me with all your heart." – Jeremiah 29:14. The Bible also says, "Draw near to God, and He will draw near to you." – James 4:8.

As we talk about leaning onto the Lord, we have to think about what it means to "pursue Christ" and "to draw near to Him." Drawing near to Him means to bring your heart to God; for instance, reading the Bible allows us to know Christ in a deeper way, prayer allows us to talk to God and receive from Him. I don't care how long we've been saved, we need to read our Bible. We are ever-growing as believers in Christ, no matter how spiritually mature we become.

We only know the part that's been revealed. We only know as much as we know. But then there's so much to the Word of God that as you continue to seek the revelation of the Word of God, you find layers to its truths and principles. It's a deep book; we'll be learning through the Word until the day we are resurrected, or we die. I should say that if we keep learning the Word of God, it will keep unfolding itself into every facet of our lives. To lean onto God is to embrace the relationship with the Word of God that we may come into the knowledge of Jesus Christ. He could then reveal himself as we walk with Him in our daily journey. Jesus discusses in the first chapter of the Book of Acts that we will receive power after the Holy Ghost has come upon us and that we should be witnesses to the whole world. This means that the Holy Ghost is the power source to witness, but that same power source ignites within us burning compassion for evangelism and passion for Christ. It causes us to fall in love with Jesus, the Father, the Holy Ghost and to embrace the reality of their love, activity, and interactions in our lives. I'm talking about intimacy for individual strength, spiritual growth, and your relationship with God, which is the foundation of your life.

As we study the Word of God and form an intimacy through God's word, the promises of God in the scripture are revealed. When you form an intimate relationship with God, through the Word of God, He unfolds and reveals His word, which roots and grounds us in the truth and gives soundness in our faith. When someone goes to teach something contrary to God's word, you're enabled to stand flat-footed on God's Word, and not be moved or swayed with every wind of doctrine. To lean onto God is when we know the Word of God because when you know the word of God, you believe in what God said He would do, what He would be to you, and who the comforter would be to you.

Walking in the Spirit solicits a mind to pray along with studying God's Word. Because if you stand on God's Word, God is going to bring it to pass. Acquire full confidence and thrust forward in the Word of God. Have full assurance that God's Word won't collapse. Live the Word by walking in the Spirit. It will be a foundation to survive the storms of life. Remember, He doesn't remove every trial, He moves us into maturity, and develops our strength, so we can endure the trial and grow our faith and our hearts. God is ever-present to help us in time of trouble. We're able to lean onto God in prayer. And in that place of prayer, we rest in His bosom, knowing that the love of God, the grace of God, and the compassion of God will comfort us. So when we get up off of our knees in prayer, our burdens erode away. I'm not talking about the physical burden, but that of the heart, soul, and spirit, where we carry the burdens of life.

God will reveal His will through the trial. God will reveal what we need to learn, where we need to be increased, and cut back. Through prayer, we have the comfort of God – the Holy Spirit - to hold us while God purges us. The Word of God is also God's communication to us. However, prayer is an invocation that allows you to talk to God and feel His presence and what God reveal to us.

Prayer is indeed a powerful thing. When we lean into praying, we find strength for the spirit and hope for tomorrow. When you read the Bible and lean onto prayer, you become a force to be reckoned with. When we put prayer and faith in the Word of God together, we're able to endure any trial and tribulation. Moreover, we're able to see the light at the end of the tunnel. You fortify mentally, become sound in understanding and in doctrine, and then the anointing will come upon that word life and on that prayer life and cause an individual to be anointed with the presence and authority of God. It's important to combine both prayer and the Word of God together. Reading the Bible in the Spirit causes transformation of your spirit as it begins to read you, revealing where you are in God, your level of spiritual maturity, and how you line up to God's Word. The Holy Spirit will unction hungry seekers to walk in the Spirit. This is when transformation happens to make the passage from conviction to conversion and from living in the flesh into living in the Spirit. Resultantly, you'll be fortified in the Spirit of God and work out the will of God in your life.

Through prayer, we learn how to live and thrive in the Word of God. As we read the Bible, we practice living through the Word of God, and as we pray, turning to the Lord for strength, support, wisdom, and grace, we allow the Holy Spirit to be active in our lives. Leaning onto the Holy Spirit means praying to God, believing what you read, obeying God's voice, as well as following the lead of the Spirit.

This type of response to the Holy Spirit will lead to becoming sensitized to the voice of the Holy Spirit. So, the Holy Spirit can guide you into all truth; because you're sensitive to the Word and Voice of God, He will reveal all that offends God in you as well as when you please God. All of this is the work of the Holy Spirit in the life of the believer to help us become a perfect man, in well accordance with the fullness of the statue of Jesus Christ.

You need the Holy Spirit because the Holy Spirit is the friend that sticks closer than a brother. The Holy Spirit is the one that walks hand in hand with you all the way to the grave and then will get you up on that last day. He reveals to us the mind of the Spirit, so we truly understand the will of God and be in rhythm. When walking in the Spirit, you will be effective, not only in your own life but also in the kingdom of God through the work of the Holy Spirit, I call Him the workhorse of the Trinity. Keep in mind that learning into God's Word gives you the power and strength to overcome tough situations. It will help you pass through the difficult moments when your strength has failed.

Your ability to lean on God for comfort, and doing simple practices of the devotions on a daily basis, will help you get through hard times. I've tried it, and I know it works. I've done it for over 38 years. I have lived with God and walked with God in the Spirit. It's tried and tested, and it's true. If it works for me, I'm certain it'll work for you, too.

Significance of Faith Built on God's Word

God's word is power and assures the foundation for our confidence in His presence and activity in our lives. There is the significance of a faith that is Bible-based. It is paramount for a believer's confidence in God to be grounded in biblical texts. God's Word is relevant, and using God's Word provides authority in the spirit realm. Applying the Word of God to our daily lives and ideologies will provoke His promises to erupt in our lives.

When you received the Word of God, you accepted it not as a human's word but as it is the Word of God, which is indeed at work in you, solidifying that God's Word is true and authentic. It is the absolute truth, alive in the heart of the believer who trusts in God and believes in the power and authority of the Word being written and inspired by God. It's not just some theological discourse of an occult mindset. It's the Word of God that men wrote as they were inspired by the Holy Spirit, empowering and opening up their understanding to write the Holy Scriptures. It was all God-inspired and is essential for the life and growth of the believer. The Word of God will stand forever, and its spiritual power will continue to transform lives.

"But the word of the Lord stands forever. – 1 Peter 1:25.

There's no way we can deny that the Word of God changes lives. Our transformation and conversion is evidence that God's Word is true. The Word of God provides for us as believers a wealth of understanding and empowerment. So, developing that intimate relationship with God in His Word and through

His Word empowers the life of the believer.

Grounding your faith and confidence in your position in Christ, as saved and redeemed, fortified, anchored, and established in the truth of the Scripture; not in an experience, solely, but in the solid foundation of the Word of God. When we read the Word of God, we learn how to walk with God in the authority of the Spirit, thereby learning how to please and be used of God. We deepen our faith by walking in this authority. We read in the Scripture that, *"By faith, Enoch was taken up so that he did not see death: 'He could not be found, because God had taken him away." For before he was taken, he was commended as one who pleased God." – Hebrews 11:5.*

Today, we can know with full assurance because of Scripture that we must please God; we don't have to guess about it. When we live in the Word of God, we experience the power, activity, and presence of God in our lives, verifying its authenticity. Then our very lives become evidence of the reality of God. You can't really prove it until you live and embrace it because this is by faith. As the Scripture states,

"If you can?" echoed Jesus. "All things are possible to him who believes!" – Mark 9:23.

The power of God is activated by faith. It's activated by our confidence in God, by believing in the Word of God; amen.

"Do your best to present yourself to God as one approved, a worker who does not need to be ashamed and who correctly handles the word of truth." – 2 Timothy 2:15.

Apply God's Word to your life in a way that's biblically sound or grounded, not distorting or changing it. Take the Word of God at its face value and apply the Scripture to your life, and be empowered by its reality. This requires taking in the purity of the Scriptures that the writer intended for us to understand. We must familiarize ourselves with what the writer intended for us to understand. So we know we're in line with the Word of God.

We must handle the word of truth with great respect because it is the ultimate truth and is breathed by God. We are transformed by its authority and by its power as believers. It is up to us as the believers to become strong in the Word of God, to become anchored in the Word of God, to make a decision to apply it to the way we think, and then to observe the effect and authority of the Word of God in our lives daily. This is where testimonies are born. I come out of a holiness church background that believed and applied ourselves to live a sanctified lifestyle. The gifts of the Spirit were flowing in the church community, and God's presence was primary. You have to make sure the Word in your heart is grounded in the biblical text. The Bible tells us, *"Let the word of Christ richly dwell within you as you teach and admonish one another with all wisdom, and as you sing the psalm, hymns, and spiritual songs with gratitude in your hearts to God." – Colossians 3:16.*

The Bible calls it a "two-edged sword," and it's indeed a "double-edged sword." It penetrates down to the bones to the raw of a matter, and it discerns, both in spirit and in truth, regarding what is right and what is wrong, all of which is done according to the Word of God. If you work the Word, the Word will work, but you have to work the word for the word to work.

What I mean is you have to employ God's Word in your life. The Word has to be in your heart. The very act of believing the Bible while you read it will cause the Word to be written in your heart by the Holy Spirit. And at the time you need it, the word will rise, and that discerning work of the sword of the Spirit, the Word of God, will rise to the occasion and reveal what truth is. That's why it's so crucial to have the truth of the Scripture in your heart, mind, and spirit.

"Search and read the scroll of the LORD; Not one of these will go missing, not one will lack her mate because He has ordered it by His mouth, and He will gather them by His Spirit." – Isaiah 34:16.

Your relationship with God's Word will empower your life. So, we stand in the place where we lean upon the attitudes, personalities, and instructions of the Scriptures. It will guide in how to behave at the moment, how to restrain in difficult situations, and how to bring ease to unbearable circumstances. In that way, reading the Scripture becomes our guide and an instruction manual for life. Indeed, the Scripture is the greatest life coach. The Holy Spirit is a teacher. When we lean on Him and walk with Him in an intimate relationship, He reveals the Word and teaches us.

God's word is powerful, it goes out and doesn't return on to Him. It has the power to do what it has been conditioned to do. It has the power to do what you release it to do when you declare it, proclaim it, and speak it.

"So My word that proceeds from My mouth will not return to

Me empty, but it will accomplish what I please, and it will prosper where I send it." – Isaiah 55:11.

As a person of faith grounded in the Word of God, God's word will not disappoint you. Whatever God sent His Word to do, it will happen. When you are in the will of God, led by the Spirit of God, and allow the Word of God to be active in your life, it will accomplish the very thing that God has sent it to do inside of you. When you speak it out and proclaim it, it will return back to God with increase. It will bring back a yield to you and a yield to God.

Therefore, having a relationship with the Word of God is fundamental and instrumental throughout a lifetime. It is the core and the foundation of the Christian life. It is the ultimate truth. Hold onto God's Word and walk in the Spirit of God. Heaven and earth shall pass away, but His Word shall abide forever. We know that the Word of God is Jesus Christ made of flesh. The Word of God is the Spirit of Christ. According to John, it is the very revelation of the Spirit of Christ.

The verse reads: "*In the beginning was the Word, and the Word was with God, and the Word was God."* – John 1:1. The verse further states, *"He was with God in the beginning. Through him, all things were made; without him, nothing was made that has been made. In him was life, and that life was the light of all mankind."*

We cannot separate the Spirit of the Word of God from the very presence and Spirit of Christ. So, to walk in the Word is to walk in Christ. The manifestation of the presence of Christ in your life is the ability to walk in the Word. It is the ability to live the life of Christ through Christ's in us. As Christ manifests in our lives, in the authority of His presence, working and drawing us into the perfect will of God, you and I are enabled to actualize the truth of the Scripture and make it apparent and relevant not only in our lives but in the lives of those who shall hear our testimony and see the activity of Christ.

When Jesus comes into the heart of the believer, their life is changed forever. I'll never forget when I first was saved and was praying in the Spirit and was deeply in the Spirit, sometimes praying for hours. Many times I couldn't even get up off the floor because I would be so drunk in the Spirit. One day, I was on my knees talking to God because I felt there was a massive barrier in my life that I could not get past. I felt stuck. I asked the Lord on my knees, "Lord, what is wrong? I know, there's a barrier that I can't get past." And then I had a vision of the Lord! The Lord himself is the witness that I saw it. I saw a clear vision with a Bible open in front of me and a voice that said to me, "Read," and I began to read the Word of God devotedly. He answered my prayer right away, teaching and helping me to understand that I could not be fully empowered by God or receive the fullness of maturity in Christ without reading my Bible. That moment transformed my life. I took the Word, and I began to read it. It helped me develop a more intimate relationship with God.

I would read God's word, sometimes sitting on the floor and at other times in my bedroom for hours with the Bible in my lap, reading God's Words, tears running down my face. As I was reading the Bible, the very presence of God would come into my room, and He would open up the eyes of my understanding about the Word of God, I kid you not the Spirit of God would engulf me and reveal the truth of scripture to me.

I would feel the literal WORD OF GOD coming off the page in the form of the light of God at the back of the page, illuminating my understanding. As I began to engage with God through His Word, it fulfilled me. And the walls in my heart came down. I began to grow in God in leaps and bounds. That proves my point of understanding how important it is for a believer in Jesus to have not only a relationship with God but in prayer. It is crucial to understand the significance, authority, and empowerment of the Word of God in your life. You will only be able to go so far, without the Word of God or without a relationship with your Bible.

As "*In the beginning was the Word and the Word was with God, and the Word was God.*" *– John 1:1*, it's clear that to have a relationship with God is to have one with the Word of God as well. The Bible plainly says that the Word was God. It was with God and was God, and we know that this is talking about the very identity of Christ before He was born in the flesh. Remember, you can't have a spiritually mature relationship with God if you don't have one with His Word. It's almost impossible for you to have a complete and satisfying relationship with God without having a relationship with His Word.

"You pore over the Scriptures because you presume that by them you possess eternal life. These are the very words that

testify about Me." – John 5:39. It is very plain here that Jesus is actually teaching about the significance of believing God's Word as a pathway to a relationship with Him.

When you read the word, you have to embrace it as absolute truth that leads to life. *"The Spirit gives life; the flesh profits nothing. The words I have spoken to you are spirit, and they are life."* – John 6:63.

I just want to close this chapter by presenting the reality that the Spirit gives life. Everything that you need in life, in terms of satisfaction, is possible as you embrace and employ the Word of God in your life, believing it as truth, and thus, God will manifest and reveal to you that He is God in your life. The Word of God will rise to the occasion and give you victory. The nugget of wisdom you must gather from this chapter is that Jesus loves you, and the Bible is significant for your life. You can count on the Spirit of God and learn of Him through the Word of God. As you employ the Word of God, it will bring you victory. Have faith and trust in the Lord. Enhance your spiritual life. Dig deep in God and grow deep. Plant your roots deep, and then you'll spring up into this awesome, righteous vessel of God for the world to see God through and are able to pick the fruit of the Spirit from your life.

Chapter 5: Bringing Self to God

Bringing one's self to God has to be intentional. God impressed upon me how important it is to have significant quality time with Him, despite being busy with other things. So, to bring ourselves to God must absolutely be an intentional, passionate desire of the heart. If you desire to know God, you must sit at the feet of God and eat at the mouth of God. To reap the anointing that flows from the intimate relationship with God, you will need to bring yourself to God. Calendar it - and don't let anything or fear interfere with it.

Bring your whole self to God. Make it a deliberate part of your daily schedule. Carve out quality time to be with God in a private place where you sit with Him. Discipline yourself to sit before Him and spend time listening for the voice of God. Bringing yourself to God is a spiritual responsibility for your spiritual growth and discernment of the Spirit.

You will have to plan it out. Sit down with your calendar, or with your iPhone, or whatever tool you use for tracking your schedule and for ensuring that you use your time wisely; because time is life, and you don't want to waste life. You can't afford to waste time but want your time to be targeted. Focus on, actualize and fulfill the calling of God in your life. You need to sit down with those apparatuses and decide how much time you're going to give to God. I'd like to see you making a deliberate effort to set aside some time, beginning with just half an hour. Get your Bible and a cup of preferred drink, whatever you need in the morning to get going. Now, just sit down before God. Be honest with God. Even if the issue is with the Lord, be honest about it. Bring it up to the Lord. Put it down before Him. Ask the Lord to help you understand, to give you clarity about it, give you direction, provide you with grace, give you understanding, and help you move in the right direction. After you've done that, sit, meditate, and quiet your spirit before Him. Take your mind off of everything. Rather take your mind to a heavenly oasis of intimacy with Christ, to where you just sit before the Lord, forcing your thoughts to come to terms with your time with God. Don't let your mind run off.

Teach your Spirit to listen to the voice of God. Now, it may take you a week to get to a point where you really begin to feel the Lord because He may test you to see if you're going to be consistent when it comes to meeting Him. As is, in any relationship, you have to put in the effort and work at it. Sit before the Lord and put those questions before Him. Talk to Him about them. Tell Him how they are impeding your life and how you truly feel. Ask Him to open up your understanding, so you can cope better. It's so important to talk to the Lord because so much could be going on inside us.

If you're mad at God, or you've got an issue with Him, for instance, you don't trust Him, you might find yourself backing away from God. If so, you won't be committed to your worship, prayer time, or your time of study. You will find yourself drawn away from God because you have all of these questions that you dare not verbalize because you feel like you'll offend God, but it may have some devastating impact on your spiritual life. But I want you to know, that's not the case. God wants you to bring all your queries to Him. He said,

"Cast all your anxiety on Him, because He cares for you." – 1 Peter 5:7.

And then He claimed, *"Come now, and let us reason together." – Isaiah 1:18.*

He wants us to first come to Him. He wants you to bring yourself to Him along with your issues, stresses, situations, queries. Bring everything to the Lord at that intimate time you have with Him in the morning. Now, we know intimacy flows throughout the day. So, in bringing ourselves to God, we're focused on quieting our Spirit and finding that special time where we go to God almost like a child that runs into the arms or bosoms of His parent for safety and security.

We mustn't bring ourselves to God only in difficult times. We must make it a habit or a practice of mindset, in which we abide by Him every day because we love and trust Him. Bringing ourselves to God is a purposeful act of submission to His presence. However, it's deeply rooted in the fact that you believe God is the rewarder of those who diligently seek Him. *"Cast not away there your confidence which hath great recompense of reward." – Hebrews 10:35.* The verse goes on, *"You need to persevere so that after you have done the will of God, you will receive what He has promised." – Hebrews 10:36.*

When we bring ourselves to God, we're coming in confidence that will birth in our spiritual competence. Wherever you are in the Lord, just come to God as is. You may come on one finger and toe, crawling up to Him, barely getting to the presence of the Lord. This means that bringing ourselves to God is actually turning inward, deciding to not be caught up in the worry of the day, to not be preoccupied with our daily struggles, stresses, passions, jobs, current circumstances, or dilemmas. Whatever it may be, the Bible says for us to bring ourselves to Him.

"Draw night to God and He will draw nigh to you." James 4:8.

When we come to Him, we are taking steps toward walking the Spirit. Or, as we learn to walk in the Spirit, we learn to come to Him and abide by Him24/7. We turn inward, and we seek the Lord's face. We turn inwards because He not only dwells up above, but He dwells in our hearts, too. "*Behold, I stand at the door, and knock: if any man hears my voice, and opens the door, I will come to Him, and will sup with him." - Revelation 3:20.*

Turning inward is to seek God's fellowship, His counsel and direction, and to seek comfort in His Lordship, and simply to hear the will of God for living. The process of bringing yourself to the Lord begins with dealing with the anxiety of life and making a conscious decision that you won't live in your apprehensions but in faith and an intimate relationship with God.

As I said earlier, you have to make your way into the presence of God. Train your mind and Spirit. Change your behavior that may have spiritual intelligence. I'm asking you to train or teach yourself to turn inward, where God dwells, and to move into His fellowship and develop intimacy resultantly. Find that place by which your personhood can be transformed and strengthened in His presence. Don't allow things that compete against your time with God. When you should be meditating, praying, and seeking the Lord by worshipping Him or reading your Bible, you're worried about worldly affairs, which, in turn, makes you tense about your lack of confidence in God. There's warfare between Spirit and faith. When you do a deliberate act of bringing yourself to God, you wholeheartedly accept that God is your ultimate resource, that He is your battle-ax to solve all your problems.

He will strengthen and provide wisdom, the right direction, revelation, and the ability to move forward in full confidence. However, it's about intentionality. Without the partnership with God, the desired change won't happen. Your prayer will work because you came to God. You declare your victory of faith because you believe that God can and will help you. Not because you're in a precarious situation, but because you walk with God in partnership for your life.

Due to that, you have an authority in His name to declare your victory in every situation. Hence, it's pertinent to bring yourself to God, so you can be led by the Spirit of God and become more sensitive to the voice of God. With God in your heart and recognizing it, you can discern Him from the noise of the world. You can distinguish your voice from God's voice and all those other voices that want to direct you. He uses people you are surrounded by – family, friends, neighbors, teachers, pastors, the fivefold ministry – to help you get closer to Him. But I'm talking about building an intimate relationship with God where you sit at the feet of God or at the throne of God and talk to Him. Be more intimate to Him than your spouse, caregivers, siblings, children, or any other loved one. He must come first. Your relationship with God must be connected to your soul and spirit so that you are united as one. As Jesus said, *"That they all may be one; as thou, Father, art in me, and I in thee, that they also may be one in us: that the world may believe that thou hast sent me." And the glory which thou gavest me I have given them; that they may be one, even as we are one." – John 17: 21 – 22.*

God wants us to be one with Him and to walk in the unity of the Spirit. Not only in the blessing and the giftedness of the Body of Christ and the fivefold ministry working in our lives, but also in bringing ourselves to God in an intimate way; so that we sit at the feet of Jesus, whether we are in the church, reading our Bible, hearing the pastor preach the prophetic word or we are simply in worship. Find your place of intimacy and connect with God. When you worship, listen to the pastor talk, or in the church, focus on the Word of God and what He is saying to your heart. Listen intently to what the man or woman of God is saying. You then apply His words to your life and make each day a more empowered living. Bringing yourself to God is a lifestyle change by which you reflect on your life and ease your worries and discomforts.

You experience a change in your behavior as you become more reflective of walking in the Spirit conquering the impulses of the flesh. Rather, you are acknowledging the Lord and all of the ways in which He directs thy path. Allow God the preeminent influence in your life. He will direct and guide you and be influential in your decision-making. There's no greater decision than that made for you in agreement with God. You see it happening when you allow God to be the wisdom of your life, have an unimaginable influence of Him in your life, spend time dwelling in the secret place, and that you live your life out of place with God. Set your heart to God!

"Say to the Lord, *I know nothing without you. But you're an all-knowing God. You have all the power, authority, and knowledge. I humble myself, to your knowledge, I surrender to the wisdom of your Spirit. And I realize that my knowledge, intellect, and experiences, though may be relevant in the world, in comparison to yours, is nothing. So, I surrender myself to you."*

Paul stated, *"More than that, I count all things as loss compared to the surpassing excellence of knowing Christ. Jesus, my Lord, for whom I have lost all things. I consider them rubbish, that I may gain Christ." – Philippians 3:8.*

One of the practices I'd like to share with you is to set up a ritual every morning for half an hour to meet with God. Indulge in the power of intimacy with Christ. Make a pattern of behavior to where you meet God every morning. The amazing part is that God will be there. He is faithful to His believers. We may not want to get out of bed in the morning and use that time to get a couple of more snoozes, but if you discipline and train yourself to get up and spend quality time with God, where you get out of the bed at a time when it's quiet and peaceful. You can read the Bible, pray, worship, and have a one-to-one conversation with God. If you want to practice meeting God or wish to develop a pattern, you need to designate a time. It could be at five o'clock in the morning, or six o'clock in the morning, or whatever works for you. It's going to be at the top of your day, not at the bottom, because you will be more attentive and strengthened to communicate with God early in the morning. So, God can transform it and influence it to bring forth in your life. Practice it over a period of a week, and then I want you to practice it for the rest of your life.

During your first times, when you've made the sacrifice of getting up early and getting with God, it's possible that at first, you may sit there, and He doesn't show up right away or the first day in terms of feeling His presence. Don't lose hope and quit. Keep coming to Him. Don't quit in one, two, or three days. Keep bringing yourself to God. Try it every day. At one point, you will start feeling the presence of God. He will eventually come to meet you. Sometimes he tries us to see if we will be faithful.

However, if you missed a morning, perhaps, you overslept or were tired the night before; after you've done this intimate practice for a week or two, you will find the Spirit of God nudging you to get up at the time you were getting up to pray, this is your confirmation that God was paying attention to you and was present, but He hid himself while you proved your faithfulness. At your weak moment, He woke you up to help you continue. He will remind you that you have time with Him. Seeing God inviting you to meet Him brings such exuberant joy because you realize that God is indeed there with you. I remember when that happened to me for the first time. I had been praying for about a week, and I was just going faithfully each morning, sitting before the Lord and reading my Bible. Initially, I didn't have any great or special encounter with the Holy Spirit. I would still show up reading my Bible in the quietness of the morning. It was beautiful, taking in the sanctity of that time. God had not made a real visit yet, so it would be just me and my sacrifice. I vividly remember that one morning, I woke up but didn't really want to get out of my bed. I woke up at my usual time because our body gets used to waking up at a set time after a while.

I couldn't bring myself to get up and go. I kind of just laid there. I didn't feel like I wanted to get out of bed that morning. So, I drifted back off to sleep in about 10 minutes or so after the time I normally woke up to be with God. To my surprise, the Spirit of the Lord woke me up. He literally called my name and woke me up. As I opened my eyes, nobody was there in the room. I felt an intense presence of God, saying to me calmly, "it's our time together."

I will never forget how much of an epiphany that was for me to understand that this was not about me feeling the presence of God at that particular time but faithfulness to it. It was about my faithfulness and consistency with God. It was about me keeping the commitment that I had made to my spiritual growth and my desire to be with God. God met me in my commitment at a time when I was weak. He woke me up. He reminded me of the commitment I had with Him. He gave me the strength to get up and meet with Him. Demonstrate your intense desire as a believer or seeker to bring yourself to God. It begins with an ambition for more of God to come into a greater knowledge of Him. An essential point that I'm trying to get across is that you have to make the decision that you're willing to sacrifice. Once you get up, drag yourself out of your bedroom to your living room or into a private place if married where you and God can have some private time together. Make the sacrifice, and you will realize that it was worth it. It will ultimately change your life.

Initially, it may feel like nothing is happening, as if you're making the sacrifice in vain. You may not immediately experience any impact of it, but you will. As you're going through your day, you will feel more influence from God in your life activities. Your ear will become more fine-tuned as the Lord brings scriptures to your mind or a song of praise to sensitize your Spirit to His presence. You will begin to feel the Spirit of the Lord becoming more active in your life, and you'll find yourself being in control of your tongue or attitude more than before. It is because the Lord manifests Himself to the believer in the simplicity of the day and in different ways.

It is in our intentional effort to pay attention to the presence and the activity of God, moving in our life every day that reveals His presence. It's in small things as well in the supernatural presence of God. When you should have made the left turn but felt compelled to go the other direction, and then you drive down the block and discover you avoided an accident. It was the leading of the Lord. It is God training your ear and heart to obey

His leading. You'll find it intensifying and becoming more vibrant in your life as you bring yourself to God. He works the way He chooses, He is God.

The key is to understand that the process requires intentional awareness. You have to commit in order for the change to happen. It will demand a deliberate act of worship and sacrifice of a mindset by which you begin to practice the simple devotions and commit yourself to what it means to walk with God. He is awesome. He is a loving savior as the Bible says,

"If you draw nigh to God, and He will draw nigh to you."- James 4:8.

All it takes is to make the decision to come under the wings of God for living. Simply put, it's just taking that spiritual step of putting God first and coming to know Him by following. Sometimes, we're so busy trying to meet our daily tasks and fulfill other people's needs that we overlook the greatness of an intentional relationship with God. Don't become so busy and overwhelmed with other activities and meeting the needs and demands of other people that you have no time for God.

When we do that, it means we put God at the end of the line. He loves us just like we love others and wants to spend time with us. And He wants us to have that time with him. Spend time with the Lord at the outset of the day. It will contribute to your success. This act of developing an intimate connection with God is possible for every believer. However, it's just a matter of deciding that you want more and you won't settle for being a mediocre Christian.

God Is A Safe Place

We have to, as the people of God, know how to tap into that secret place with God and have the discernment to see what God is saying and doing.

Secondly, your relationship with God is your place of safety. It is a place where you can find safety in difficult seasons for your emotional health, mental health, as well as your physical health. God is faithful to your whole being. And lastly, I want you to grow your spiritual self, meaning, develop a deeper partnership with God in these difficult seasons, to grow your spiritual self. Be encouraged and trust the Lord as your Savior and your Redeemer. Understand that God is with you. He said,

"I will never leave you nor forsake you." – Hebrew 13:5.

He will be with us always. He'll never leave you without His intervention and empowerment to survive the times. He'll never leave you in a situation where you can't hide in Him until the wind blows over. Nestle down inside of God and find the safety and security that's in Jesus Christ; by faith, you must believe that God can and will keep you. You must believe that God will sustain you. Like the children of Israel in the book of Exodus, you must believe that God will take care of you in the wilderness seasons of your life.

God will keep you forever if you yield to be kept. While you learn to trust Him, it is the streamlining of the Holy Ghost and the activity of God in our lives that causes us to know God more intimately and deeply. If we can discern the hand of God and become intentional and attentive to what God is saying to us at the moment, we are hidden in the Holy Ghost for spiritual development and our survival. Ask the Lord to nurture your spiritual mind, in fact, your whole spiritual self, so you're able to hear the voice of God, discern the work of God, embrace the Word of God, and apply His Word to your situation.

When you apply the Word to understand why God is working the way He is working in your life, you grow in the specific area that God has designed for your growth. He uses life situations, including our trials and tribulations, to grow our character and spiritual intellect, and improve our mental and emotional health. We must understand that walking with God is a full life experience. It's not just compartmentalized into your praise, worship, and Bible study time, it is a journey. He is the God of your entire life.

In those difficult moments, when you have no power and authority to change your circumstance, God wants you to understand He is your safe place and a place of refuge. When you can find your way to God in those precarious moments, just be real, honest, and open to hearing His will.

Make sure you go in your sincere heart and ask the Lord to help you, and ask Him to open up the eyes of your understanding, and to give you discernment, so you can hear His voice when He's speaking and discern His hand when He's moving, and to embrace His Spirit when He's communing with you. God is calling you to a place of maturity, to be confident in His faithfulness; where you have a spiritual IQ that centers you in faith and astuteness to God. I've had to run into God and find safety in Him to be spiritually competent to overcome the challenges and difficulties in my life. Similarly, I ran into the Lord during a rough patch and found safety for my entire life. I was spiritually healed, and He taught me to trust His Word, quote it and believe it to take authority over the situation.

"I believe in God's Word, and I can apply this Word to this situation. I stand against failure. I resist failure. I refuse to lose. But rather I'm standing on the promises of God and those promises in themselves is enough to give me the courage and confidence to walk out of a trial victoriously."

By doing this, you will find yourself strengthened. What I am saying is the proclamation of faith is a powerful tool you need to exercise in times of fear and spiritual warfare. It is a weapon of faith that overcomes the tricks and deception of the enemy of our soul.

Now here's the revelation, once you allow God to be your confidant, protector, and provider, you will freely lean onto Him in those unfavorable seasons. He will become such a part of who you are that you will automatically begin to lean onto Him. You'll trust Him. And you will tap into the love of God and believe that God's love and His grace are sufficient for you in any season. You ground your faith and hope in God when you stand up to opposition with spiritual tools provided by God in His Word. Paul states in the King James Bible,

"I know both how to be abased, and I know how to abound: everywhere and in all things I am instructed both to be full and to be hungry, both to abound and to suffer need." – *Philippians 4:12.* This verse is crucial for every believer looking to learn how to abide by God. It can be scary when the terrain or life cycle changes and things don't look like your norm, and you are in an unfamiliar situation. When we have testimonies of His faithfulness and have been a witness to His everlasting love in awkward seasons, we learn to feel safe in Him. Being steady in these seasons is crucial for you to make it to the end of your journey.

This will allow you to enter that place of safety, where your full confidence in God becomes your place of safety, where you find peace in troubled times, and you're able to have a settled spirit; because you know that God is who He says He is. And you know that God will do what He said He would do. You also know that God will do it for you and that you are secure in Christ Jesus.

When you believe that He is faithful despite what it feels like, you can stand on the truth of the Scripture, which states clearly, *"The Lord is faithful, who will establish you and guard you from the evil one." – Thessalonians 3:3.* God is indeed faithful; you can embrace and hold on to Him. Even if your knees are wobbling, your heart is racing; your hands are jittery, stand on the promises of God's Word, and hold God's Word true.

Though you may not understand the season you are in, still trust God. Take courage and proclaim, "I will trust you through the storm. I will trust you when I don't understand. I will trust you when it's an unfamiliar place because I know you are a faithful God. And I know you will be with me, even to the ends of the world. I know that your faithfulness is present in this situation and for the rest of my life because there's nothing in this world that you cannot conquer." God sometimes leads us the long way around to grow us, but trust God to do in you what is needed for you to love Him and not quit in seasons of difficulty. He knows how to deepen you. In times like these, hold onto the verse in Exodus 13,

"Then it came to pass, when Pharaoh had let the people go, that God did not lead them by way of the land of the Philistines, although that was near; for God said, "Lest perhaps the people change their minds when they see war and return to Egypt." So God led the people around by way of the wilderness of the Red Sea. And the children of Israel went up in orderly ranks out of the land of Egypt."

God did not lead them by way of the land of the Philistines, although it was closer: The coastal route was the shortest way to go from Egypt to Canaan. God knew the people of Israel were not ready to face this yet, and they may change their minds when they see war and return to Egypt, so He led them a different way. It doesn't matter how the storm may seem to increase or how it may seem to rage; God will bring you out just like He did with Israel over and over again in the biblical text. He's a safe place even when storms are raging. We can hide inside of God and find protection. No matter what the trial, anchor yourself in God in Christ, and you will always come out victorious.

We must learn to trust God, no matter what the intensity of the trial is, no matter how tough the circumstances are, no matter how God makes us wait before He answers. Again, I say, wait. We want to trust the Lord, regardless of what it feels or looks like. When we take on the courage to trust God, He will get in the midst of it, and the Holy Spirit will be with you. He will sustain you. The Holy Spirit will fortify and strengthen you. He will grow your faith in Him to another level.

From time to time, we have to go back and ask Him for new strength for the next phase in life. Finding safety in God is about knowing that the Lord is the place of your restoration. He's where we find recovery and healing. If you are attentive to God, you will be tuned in to His Spirit and be in rhythm with Him; you're enabled to hear what God has to say to you. You can understand what is needed and what God has for you at the moment, propelling you to the next step in your life. He'll never ignore your needs if you trust in Him.

If we turn to Him in prayer, force our heart and Spirit to rest in God, build intimacy with Him, and allow Him to do the work in you. He may give you the Word, hover His Spirit over you while you are in prayer and comfort you, and give revelation. The thing is to get into the presence of God, so you can secure that place where there's strength, power, and authority to protect you, your now and your tomorrow, your destiny, and your overall life. He can secure your tomorrow. God can do anything. The Scripture says,

"Now to Him who is able to do so much more than all we ask or imagine, according to His power that is at work within us." – Ephesians 3:20

Note that the power that works within us is the power of God ignited by faith with tenacious intentionality and causes us to force our way into victory. However, we have to believe our way into it and through it. With each step you take, trust God and His Word to be true. Believe that God will do what He said He would. And that's the key thing – to believe that God has all the power and authority in this world and beyond. Use those resources of God made available to the believer through relationship with Christ, fueled and funneled into your life activities, in your conversations, finances, businesses, and so on.

Watch God be God; watch Him do phenomenal work that you only dreamed He could do. Watch God be God in your life because He wants to be glorified; and He wants to give you a praise point. What do I mean by a praise point? I mean, the Lord wants you to focus on what He's done in your life so powerful that it causes you to pause and praise Him. This means that a praise point is a form of positive praise you give at the moment when you witness God's glory in your life. And that praise is so powerful that it bursts within you. It fills you with joy, peace, and satisfaction. Believe me, God is going to come on time, but you have to believe it. We have to train our spirits to trust the Lord and not be tricked by the anxiety or any other emotion that arises in such situations to cheat our faith.

Most importantly, remember the last praise point and last victory that God gave you. Don't forget who God is. Go back to His Word and find those scriptures that relate to your situation. If you take notes or do journaling, start writing down what God is doing in your life and what you think that God has done in your life. Every once in a while, go back and read them; they'll give you the confidence for tomorrow. They'll help you get through the difficult moments because your confidence in God will be solidified. It will help you remember all that God has done because he's been faithful in your life. He's that kind of God. He's always loyal and is faithful in the life of the believer.

The Bible states,

"For I know the plans I have for you," declares the Lord, "plans to prosper you and not to harm you, plans to give you a hope and a future." – Jeremiah 29:11.

In partnership with God, you will become a strong person that loves God. You will be fully equipped to make it through the times when they feel unbearable. When you walk in the Spirit, He will teach you how to wait and grow your faith in God. He will not let you hit bottom like the eagle when she is teaching her younglings to fly. She pushes them off the nest. And when they started plunging down the mountain, she shoots down and bare them up on her wings. God states,

"You have seen for yourselves what I did to Egypt, and how I carried you on eagles' wings and brought you to Myself." – Exodus 19:4.

Be encouraged and know that the Lord loves you.

Chapter 6: Prayer and God's Promises

In this chapter, we'll focus on prayer and God's promises. There are promises that are a part of the outflow of the salvation experience. In a nutshell, communication from the heart to the ears of God results in the grace and intervention of the Holy Spirit in believers' lives. The scripture states throughout them that the outcome of prayer are miracles, God's intervention, reformation, transformation, and the empowering of faith.

"The effectual fervent prayer of a righteous man availeth, much" – James 5:16

Hence, it is so important to understand the value and the power of prayer. It's like a rocket - out of the heart and mind of the believer into the hearing of God. God's resources for the Body of Christ are maintained in the heavenly storehouse of God, and prayer pulls out of the spiritual realm into the natural realm. God Knows you and has tailored resources for your life experience, and through your authentic on-time prayer, God's plan for your expected end is magnetized to the provision of God for His will to actualize in you, your life, and those you are to minister to. Prayer is heart language coupled with need and desire and is our method of spiritual communication with God.

All the riches and wealth that you need to be effective in ministry are already laid up in heaven for you. Prayer is the way to access them. Prayer is usually manifested in timing with our readiness in alignment with God's will so that we maximize the fulfilment of God's work through us. We must develop the ability to wait on the season we're supposed to have it; there's a specific season in which those answered prayers unveil in our lives, but I must include that sometimes prayers are also instantaneous. At other times, we're not ready for it. I'm a firm believer that when God sends the answer to prayer, He shapes or forms it to fit our lives for the next growth opportunity.

Answered prayer should ignite praise and a heart of worship because God's infinite wisdom is revealed in our answered prayer. As our understanding is expanded we learn how to identify the work of God in us as well as through us. The growth moment and call of God to maturity is revealed through answered prayer. Herein is the privilege and opportunity to grow our faith and increase our ability to discern God's love toward us.

We must trust God and allow Him to provide us with the opportunity. Be content in the fact that God will answer your prayer. We just have to trust the Lord. When we get up off of our knees, we're supposed to know with full assurance that God not only has heard our prayer but that He is going to answer it in the fullness of time.

It doesn't matter what the situation is or how strong the opposition to the prayer is, learning to pray anyway and to anticipate spiritual growth as we sit before God is a good process for discerning God's activity in your life and ministry. Effective prayer is the prayer that won't surrender its hope in the time of opposition but rather sharpens its intention to win regardless of what challenges present themselves. This happens when confidence is grounded in God's ability to answer the prayer. When you know that God hears and receives your prayer and that He will ultimately respond in the most suitable time, doubt becomes insignificant. See, faith waters peace and stabilizes the emotional state of those that believe to the point of refusing to be denied. This mindset is tenacious in its pursuit of God.

It reminds me of the scripture when the man of God prayed, and the angel responded to him, "God heard you when you first prayed, but He was hindered by Satan. And the angel was fighting the battle for the believer to get that prayer." Daniel 10:12-14. God is so powerful and in complete control that nothing can prevent him; therefore, an answer to prayer happens at the time that it is supposed to. The issue is to stay hopeful during the waiting period, strengthening your ability to hold on through the night, trusting that God is going to do it.

When God aligns your prayer with purpose, you will never forget it, and it will birth something new and fresh within you, erupting into a heart of worship in acknowledgement that God is sovereign. This brings the revelation, knowledge of the power and the love of God in the life of the believer. God is revealed in us through answered prayer. When He is revealed to us through answered prayer, we are to respond to that revelation of God with total surrender to His will.

Answered prayer increases our confidence in God. He will then build us up in our most holy faith, that we may be empowered to walk with Him in full authority. Prayers, faith, and the promises of God work together as a trinity of victory. Hence, prayer is a powerful spiritual attitude that provokes the presence and the hand of God in our lives.

I believe in trifold devotion – a union between the heart, head, and our hands by which a believer works in unity with the Spirit of God. We need our hearts to be authentic and genuine toward God. We need our heads to understand the will of God and solicit our effort toward God, forcing spiritual intelligence for submitting to growing in God. Meaning we use our intellect and understanding to comprehend the things of God. We need our hands which helps us perform spiritual work, and by that, what I mean is that we put into action the revelation of God in our mind and hearts.

We also know that the prayer of the righteous is powerful and effective. We also know that the Lord's ears are attentive to the prayers of the righteous. We know that whatsoever we ask Him, we shall receive and thereby know that we must always pray and not give up in times of temptation against our faith. The scripture says, "For ye have need of patience, that, after ye have done the will of God, ye might receive the promise." – Hebrew 10:36.

The promises of God are actualized as we believe in God and trust Him to bring it to pass. Our faith in God is evident when we pray to Him because we would not pray if we did not believe that He would answer it. What you need or desire from God is provoked by prayer and gives angels permission to work on your behalf. Prayer is the manifestation of a relationship with God and leads to pleasing God and results in victory over all that does not please God in our lives. What I am saying is, when we pray, we discover the strength to become, to transform whatever lives within us that does not please him, and thereby when we yield those hindrances to God, we are empowered to force a victory over all opposition to our total wholeness in God

'The Bible says,

"When a man's ways please the LORD, he maketh even his enemies to be at peace with Him." – Proverbs 16:7.

We also know that the desires of our hearts are also brought to pass as we please God. That is why it's so important for our prayers and our expectations to be established on God's word. We must be careful to couple grace with the life of commitment to Christ because grace is in its beauty complement grace through a life of obedience to God evidenced by a life resembling the teaching of scripture.

The Bible says, "Ye shall know them by their fruits." – Mathew 7:15. Spiritual fruit is a response to grace.

Thereby, the two of them are coupled together and position us to expect answered prayer from God. The Lord is calling us – believers – to live a life that is biblically grounded. Prayer is power with God. It is purchasing power. It is the communication vehicle by which we actualize the desires of our hearts in relationship with God.

Remember, Paul was a great man in the Jewish Kingdom. He set a great example of what it meant to know God. He really did not have a relationship with Him until he was knocked from his beast by God to a posture of submission. When he received the revelation that He was encountering Jesus Christ, Paul began to pray. Jesus addresses his transformed life when he says to Ananias in the book of Acts. He prayeth now. Prayer is a posture of humility, an act of faith, and reverence of God. In response to that revelation, Paul began to pray. God speaks to this posture of prayer as evidence of Paul's conversion and His humility to God as proof that Paul was a changed man.

We know that prayer is a result of the conversion experience. We cannot say that we know God, and we don't have a prayer life. Prayer is the beginning of the act of repentance. We are strengthened as we stay in communication with God through prayer. God is calling us to pray. He is pulling the church back into prayer. We see all through scripture that it was prayer that provoked God to respond and change the conditions for Israel, the prophets, and individuals in the Bible, both Old and New Testaments.

God is calling His church back to prayer. He is calling individuals back to prayer. The question is, will we humble ourselves and pray? We want answers without sincere prayer. We've taken things into our own hands. It is time to learn how to pray and expect the promises of God. Effective praying is when an individual connects with God in sincere prayer and believes that God will do it. He believes in who He is, what He says. By faith, you understand that He is God. When we believe and anchor our prayers in God, who declared Himself as God and revealed his promises through the biblical text we find intimacy and power with and for God to our world.

Understand that effective praying is fore-mostly centered on God and in believing God will do it, without any shadow of a doubt, that God has the ability to answer your prayer. He will not allow you to be destroyed as you wait. The second part of effective praying is anchoring your confidence in the revelation of the God of the Bible. Then the third part of effective praying is the ability to patiently wait on God to bring it to pass. The Bible says many times, and I quoted this earlier, that faith demands patience to receive God's promise. For the scripture says very plainly in Hebrew, 10: 35 through 37,

"so do not throw your confidence; it will be richly rewarded. You need to persevere so that when you have done the will of God, you will receive what he has promised. For, in just a little while, he who is coming will come and will no delay."

Believe in God and trust Him for the impossible because God wants to work a miracle in your heart to solidify your core faith. As the Bible quotes:

"Now faith is confidence in what we hope for and assurance about what we do not see." Hebrews 11:1.

And without faith, it is impossible to please God, because anyone who comes to him must believe that he exists and that he rewards those who earnestly seek him." – Hebrews 11:6.

Chapter 7: Discerning the Spirit of God

A lot of people struggle with understanding how to discern the Spirit of God in their lives. They are struggling to know when God is speaking to them and if he is truly leading them to do something. In particular, that God has called them to do something. Many struggles with understanding what it feels like to hear God and discern if God is actually engaging their hearts to His cause. Discerning God's presence is a spiritual pursuit and solicits God to reveal His will to you as a seeker. As we walk intimately with God, sit at the heart of God, and surrender ourselves to the Lord, we find that God is interested in having a genuine and free-flowing, intimate relationship with us.

This intimacy is so naturally spiritual that when we are truly seeking God in the Spirit, His response to us situates us at his feet in humility. Humility is a prerequisite for hearing and surrendering to God. When we learn to quiet our lives, and we seek the face of God through prayer, quietness, and discernment of the Bible as a guide to hearing, discerning and experiencing God. We must intentionally allow God to lead us through the day. Learning to be sensitive to the Spirit of God demands respect for the teaching of the Word of God, the Bible. This reference is a posture of humility and honor for acknowledging God is a Spirit. When we sit in His presence through prayer and Bible Study, we become more sensitive to His presence as He uses faith in the Word as His voice and direction to lead us into Him.

John 4:24 KJV

24 God is a Spirit: and they that worship him must worship him in spirit and in truth.

Since God is a Spirit and seeks us to worship or demonstrate reference for the fact that He is God, the ultimate spiritual being. Thus, yielding our spirits to him in a humble gesture of love and obedience to His Word, and becoming sensitive to our own spirituality and linking its health and maturity to our relationship with God is essential to come into knowing God as sovereign. His expectation of our recognition of Him as creator and the lover of our soul is necessary to learn to identify God's presence and activity in our lives.

This mindset and spiritual composure lead to spiritual discernment and spiritual maturity. Another way of saying this is: Paying attention to the clear teachings of scripture about God's identity and what he wants us to understand about Him is key to transforming our thinking to that which is spiritual instead of leaning to our own understanding about matters of the Spirit. Coming to this understanding is only possible when we humble ourselves to the Word so that the Spirit of God can soften our hearts to His voice and Spirit. We can only do this by the grace of God.

God initiates our attention to Him and what happens next depends on our response to God. This moment of opportunity is presented by God, but what we do with it will determine if you will become sensitive and learn to live in harmony and unity with God the Father, the Spirit, and the Word. This is why it is important to learn to embrace the truth and spirituality of God's Word. It is the seed of Christ to be received in our hearts, so we are enabled to discern the Spirit of God through it. Responding to God's presence when He knocks happens when we solicit and intentionally invite Him in. When we do this, He comes in with a plan to grow us up in Him and to reveal Himself as our Lord and Savior. A part of this process is to master the posture of humility.

Because He is God, we have to learn to bow and reference Him as the deity and thereby become co-dependent on His voice and Spirit. This practice is a learned discipline developed and matured as we sit in His presence, embrace the Word, and lean onto God for a deeper understanding and strength to obey it daily. As we get better at yielding to His revealed presence, we become wiser at discerning His Spirit. See, in the consistent practice of prayer and the refining of the spiritual ear to hear God, we are able to recognize Him as He advances His will in our lives and colorfully ensures we know it is Him.

Celebrating God's faithfulness and active loving care in our daily lives is spiritual, and it provokes God's presence and will toward His total plan for the Church and his world. It was all created to serve Him. As we identify and celebrate God's presence, it seems He visits more frequently and intensifies His communing with us as well as His revelation of Himself in us. Deciding to form an intimate relationship with God so that you can hear and recognize God is a step toward setting the scene for a visit from God. Doing the spiritual work of self-reflection, separation from all that hinders your hearing of God is crucial to learning to choose Him over everything else. Live life so sensitive to the presence of God that you hear God when He speaks. This means learning to quiet your spirit and teach it to be open to Him when reading your Bible, when bowing in prayer and when hearing the preached or taught Word of God. Choosing to put your relationship with God first and actively weeding out fear and doubt that can distabilize your faith will situate your spiritual effort to know Him in the presence of God. We are called to become close to God, and in pursuit of Him, we learn what His will is for our lives. Discerning spiritual things come through spending time in His presence as well as openness to deepening our understanding of what the will of God is for His people.

The foundation of discovering what God is doing in you directly relates to a heart surrendered to God. We must want this to have this! Intimacy is developed through authentic, heart yielded prayer that grows into a deepened faith in God and then manifest in us through His activity . I must say that prayer is the core foundation for learning to walk in the Spirit. I'm not talking about the rewards of prayer. I'm talking about bringing your heart to God. Imagine sitting at the feet of God and crawling up in the lap of God for closer proximity.

If you can just envision that in your mind, you will realize that in His presence is shelter and protection from all that keeps you in the flesh. Living in the Spirit is an acknowledgement that we are weak in comparison to the power that flows from walking in the Spirit with God. Try it and discover the powerful love and presence of God liberating you from every distraction that is keeping you away from the revelation of His presence. It's a choice to know God in the Spirit and to give yourself to Him for becoming Spirit. Practice this by hiding in the Spirit. Hiding in the Spirit is a deliberate giving of oneself to Him. Talk to God out of your heart, holding nothing back, and then quietly pay attention to His presence. Don't get ahead of Him with a lot of expectations but rather simply wait and embrace Him. He is a loving, warm and comforting presence. Sit down quietly in His presence, go inside your heart, and begin to communicate with God in a love language that comprises of words of thanksgiving. Love language with God provokes the response of God in you and teaches you how to hear God's voice. As the Bible says,

"No one can come to Me unless the Father who sent Me draws him, and I will raise him up at the last days." – John 6:44.

It means that God does the solicitation; we just have to respond sincerely. He helps us do so by allowing us to enjoy the warmth. When you begin to walk in intimacy with God, you've already been drawn by God to come to Him. All we're doing is responding to the Courtship of God, to the solicitation of the Holy Spirit for our humility in service.

In the beginning stages of discerning the Spirit of God is to be attentive to God's presence in pursuit of Him. My meeting place with God was my bathroom. I had at this time young children, and so I would use their nap time to close up in the bathroom as my prayer closet and spend my time in God's presence. I learned to discern God's presence here through prayer. It is teaching oneself to be sensitive and attentive by quieting the spirit and denying yourself busyness. Learning to discern God's Spirit begins when you learn to tune out all those voices that dominate your life and intentionally meditate on the Word. Learning to discern God's presence is a process and does not happen immediately. However, it happens as we desire to know Him and position ourselves to be sensitive to the Spirit. Becoming sensitive to the Spirit is separation from the flesh in mind, heart, and spirit. It is an intentional discipline to hear God and to recognize His activity in your life by discerning the difference between your voice, other's voices, your work, and God's activity in your life and thereby acknowledging God as active.

Pay attention and spend time in worship and prayer so you can get in touch with how God responds to your praise, your prayer, and your worship. Then master your surrendering to God and discover what provokes God to manifest himself to you. I can tell you that authentic prayer and worship are a magnet to God's presence. The honesty of heart and going on the inside of your heart to feel God is powerful and requires patience. But you can feel Him if you are able to quiet your spirit before Him, He will reveal Himself. Another way is to believe God's Word and to apply it to your life and watching God work. These are some of the ways that you can begin to provoke your discernment of the Spirit of God.

Intentionality is necessary to discern God's Spirit in your life. It is sometimes easier in the corporate setting to see God at work by those who spend time soliciting God's presence through a sold-out life of love, faith, and obedience. This is not learned overnight but is a day-by-day growth process, and God gets in it with you and helps to recognize His Spirit as He wants us to know Him. After a while, you'll learn how to be into God and develop an intimacy with Him. At the foundation of establishing an intimate relationship with God, you have to quiet your life, surroundings, and, most importantly, your mind so that you can appropriately discern Him. He is waiting on your commitment to Him, so He can reveal He is God and teach you to walk in the Spirit. For walking in the Spirit requires discipline, daily commitment, a sort of desperation for God that drives your heart to Him and courts you into His very presence.

Deciding to live a life in the discernment of the Spirit is an on-purpose mindset. This choice also includes responding to His call to spend time with Him, to walk with Him in the Spirit so He can teach you about eternal things that reveal God and His love for you and his world. Really, it is to pay attention to the presence of God in your life and acknowledge His presence and yield yourself to Him without hesitation, and as you practice this, He will draw you closer to Him. Many times in my life, when God has provoked a conversation with me, it's been in the wee hours of the night when I'd be lying in my bed, and I'd feel the strong presence of God enter the room. Undeniable it was Him. His love and warmth are so full of comfort and sometimes intense alertness and desire to hear. God's presence is a revelation for discerning God's will. In those times, I conversed with God, saying, "Yes, Lord, what is it that you want me to do or simply was just quiet to hear? And I quite myself before God so I could hear Him and to be in His presence. Be tenacious about it. Remain protective over it, like a lion is over her cub."

Discipline yourself to sit with God, even if He just hovers. Just sit there in His presence. It is so good for your soul, like a cleansing. Initially, you may want to say, "Lord, I'm here to hear your voice. I'm here to hear your will. Lord, help me to yield and quieten myself according to your will." You will discern when you are to say nothing when the words won't come, and maybe just tears or worship flows instead. Go with it, follow God in the Spirit.

Don't be disheartened if you are fearful the first few times as it is supernatural. Be consistent with your practice to surrender to God. If you do, you are going to start feeling God's presence more and more as you learn to yield and discern Him. I remember my first time; when I really felt the Spirit of God. He came in to have fellowship with me. At that moment, I was afraid. And we know that's not uncommon because of John in the isle of Patmos. The Bible mentions in the book of revelations, the first chapter, that John fell to his knees in fear at the presence of God. He had to be strengthened to stand before God. He is God, so yes, it can be fearful, but as you spend time with Him and teach yourself to trust, God will help you build trust, and the fear will lift.

Revelation 1:17-18 KJV

[17] And when I saw him, I fell at his feet as dead. And he laid his right hand upon me, saying unto me, Fear not; I am the first and the last:

[18] I am he that liveth, and was dead; and, behold, I am alive forevermore, Amen; and have the keys of hell and of death.

Wrestle your fear to the mat and say out loud, "I won't be afraid, God. I won't let fear of the unknown hinder me, God." And then ask God to give you strength. I remember when the first time it happened to me, I shut down immediately. I came out of that place because I was fearful. I ran out of the Spirit and resisted God's presence by not praying too deeply. It took me a while until I came back to God with a depth of seeking again. But then, my spirit longed for the presence that I had felt.

Even though I was afraid, my spirit was so hungry to be in the presence of God again. I had felt His warmth and love in a more intense way than ever, except when I received the baptism of the Holy Spirit. I believe the Lord let me miss Him to develop the longing for Him enough to risk it all to be in His presence; so that I would want Him enough to push beyond fear. I had to learn how to trust and yield to God so He could reveal Himself in the Spirit. I couldn't be more grateful.

As we begin to pursue a real intimate relationship with God – the one that fills us with His Spirit and upon our acceptance of Him, he comes into our heart – thank you, Jesus! When we yield to the Spirit of the Living God, He manifests Himself in our lives. As you pursue God with sincerity, He will meet you in that quiet place. He will begin to manifest Himself as God, and He will begin to reveal the will of God in your life. He'll teach you the Word of God and open up your understanding, and thereby you will help you to discern the Spirit of God in your life.

Chapter 8: The Power of the Word of God

The Word of God is Spiritual and is powerful and transforms the mind, spirit, and heart of those hungry to walk with God. When you begin to read your Bible with a spiritual mind and heart, the Word will plant itself in your heart as God has already commissioned it to do. The Word of God is Spirit, and it is transforming power in the life of the believer. The one who believes and applies it to their thinking and living will be transformed by it. It is so real, and while you're reading, its power will convert our thinking system to that of faith in God. The effect of His Word is the power to walk in the Spirit.

Our confidence in the power of scripture and its inspiration from God centers it as the core of our faith. Hearing God's Word or the Bible is to begin to hear what God is saying to you and His world. However, coming to understand God's call to us is to authenticate that God's Word is the ultimate truth. This truth is absolute, and there is no failure in it. Because it is truth that holds power to transform our inner man to serve God. Being trained by the Spirit of God to hear the Word is life-transforming. It is the privilege of a lifetime and leads to spiritual maturity. Spending time in the Word builds faith and refines our hearing.

Romans 10:17 KJV

17 So then faith cometh by hearing, and hearing by the word of God.

As we learn to discern God's presence and commit to learning the Word of God, we discover how God engages us and how we are to approach Him. God's Word is alive, and when we embrace it as truth, we can feel the power of it as it transforms our thoughts, emotional life and empowers us for a deepened intimacy with God. You can feel the impartation of the Word of God coming on the inside of you and then beginning to manifest the authority of God in you. When you wonder what God is doing in you, you will begin to see with clarity that God is moving in your life.

The Spirit of God, even as I'm writing, is moving my mind to tell you how significant it is for you to allow God in your space, to welcome Him to come into your heart, and to be real in you. He wants you to get beyond the fear of the supernatural and allow Him to come into your life. So, He can speak to you as well as lead and guide you into all truth. Don't be afraid of being in quiet places with God. Don't be scared of the supernatural presence of God. Don't be afraid of being afraid. Allow the Lord to be your God.

Allow Him to manifest Himself in your life, and let Him deal with you in a supernatural way. He is provoking you to intimacy and experiencing the reality of the work of the Cross and the love of God that has been manifested toward you in Jesus Christ. As you develop intimacy and relish your relationship with God, you will see the love of God actualizing in you and toward those you encounter. As you encounter the Holy Spirit and you open up to Him, you learn how to be in His presence and receive the impartation of the Holy Spirit.

When the Spirit of God is in you, He heals your life scars. God manifests Himself as a Healer in your life. He's a lover of your soul and cares about you and your success in Him. He wants to be a friend that sticks closer than a brother. He wants to be the God in your life that reveals his glorious work as you live. As you move in life, the Spirit of God will use you because you've learned how to yield your life, spirit, and will to Him. Find the courage and strength to walk in the power of the Word of God and allow the Spirit of God to train you how to become your best person in Him for His will and your life empowerment. Look for that quiet place in the closet of your life – heart or mind – and sit down in the presence of God with the Bible.

The Holy Spirit will train you how to listen and discern more closely. Allow God through the study of the scripture and openness to the move of the Spirit of God to form within a keen sense of obedience to His leading. He works in partnership with our will. He won't force us to listen or obey, we must want to. Keep at it! When you enter into that secret place of your heart where you can experience that revelation for growing in God that only He can do in you. To truly find the power of the Word working in you happens when we know God's Word and are honest with ourselves and the Holy Spirit enough to obey and follow His lead. In this posture, it will become clear what God is doing in your life, as well as faith in God through believing in the power of scripture. Be willing to do adventures in God. It will be the adventure of a lifetime. However, it will require admitting wherever you lack the strength and courage to surrender yourself totally to His. Yield to the Lord and allow His love and grace to fill your spirit. He's calling you to the ultimate purpose of God and teaching you how to live in intimacy with Him. Surrender your whole being, so you can hear, feel, and experience God without hesitation. God wants to do some things in you that will blow your mind. Give you an understanding of the Word, that through the work of the Holy Spirit, there is a supernatural impartation and revelation of what the author and finisher of our faith intended you to understand.

The power of the scripture affords power through our knowledge of His Son whom He revealed, and in the revelation of Jesus Christ, we experience the manifested presence of the Father. Jesus fulfilled the Word of God and revealed its eternal existence to all who believe. He spoke it and finished its prophetic proclamation of the love of God toward His people and we affirm our will to Him through proclaiming the power of scripture in our lives. Our response to Jesus' act of love and obedience gives God an opportunity to reveal His power and affords our access to the resources of God through the revelation of His Son. The power of Word leads us to walk in the Spirit, liberating us from all bondage and fortifying the work of God as the Holy Spirit trains us to actualize in the Spirit.

Chapter 9: Next Steps

What is God doing in His people for such a time as this? When we learn to walk in the Spirit, we are positioned to move into purpose. Learning to hear and follow God's will is the precursor to walking in the Spirit. It is a lifestyle of surrender to God. The next step is preparation for what is to come and the fulfilment of that which we have learned of God for moving forward into purpose. As we discern how to walk in the Spirit, understanding the next steps is key to discerning God's will for our lives.

Discovering the next step after being filled with the Spirit of God and accepting His love and grace leading to intimacy with Him is important to what's next. God in His perfect will for each of us and His Church to the world is revealed as we center our minds and spirits to discern what God wants to do next. Not all the time does God reveal in advance through dreams and visions or simple revelation, understand that sometimes He makes us wait without clarity.

What's next is bigger than you and I. Walking in the Spirit demands a desire to continue to grow and to seek God's face for what is next, but understanding that our next and His next may be very different in terms of activity and timing. What does God want to do next? What does He want to do in and through you in the bigger picture of His will for His ministry to the world through His people? What I mean is we must be studious about what God is doing and what He has chosen for us to do in the fulfilment of His will. We must pray for the Holy Spirit to reveal it, so we get to be spiritually sensitive.

Knowing how to live in the Spirit and discerning the next steps may require fasting and praying to refine your ear to hear the Holy Spirit. Becoming larger than the possibilities of the flesh is of paramount importance. This is important to our walking in the Spirit because in the flesh, we cannot please God. We only please God by walking in the Spirit.

Romans 8:8 Context

[5]For they that are after the flesh do mind the things of the
flesh; but they that are after the Spirit the things of the
Spirit. [6]For to be carnally minded is death; but to be spiritually
minded is life and peace. [7]Because the carnal mind is enmity
against God: for it is not subject to the law of God, neither
indeed can be. ***[8]So then they that are in the flesh cannot please***
God. *[9]But ye are not in the flesh, but in the Spirit, if so be that*
the Spirit of God dwell in you. Now if any man have not the Spirit
of Christ, he is none of his. [10]And if Christ be in you, the
body is dead because of sin; but the Spirit is life because of
righteousness. [11]But if the Spirit of him that raised up Jesus from
the dead dwell in you, he that raised up Christ from the dead
shall also quicken your mortal bodies by his Spirit that dwelleth
in you.

So, walking in the Spirit is the absence of walking in the flesh. It is an intentional determination to shed the flesh and its works. This is why honesty is so important as an initial step to transition from fleshly thinking to Spiritual living. Only the one seeking this supernatural lifestyle can cross the threshold of change. It is indeed a threshold as it must be a departure and entry into the Spirit. Our willingness to embrace this transformation is what centers us at the door of change. God leads us there, but we have to choose to walk across and into the Spirit. When we have the heart to know and love God, we are ushered into the process of transformation where the Holy Spirit does his mastery work on our hearts for growing us up in the Spirit.

To walk in the Spirit is to own the reality that this is a day-to-day journey and not a sprint. It is a marathon by which the Holy Spirit is the coach and trainer and guides those seeking to master the yielding of self to God to find their greatest personhood in identity with Christ. The journey offers moments and seasons by which we are challenged to know ourselves as God does and rechannel how we process thoughts and actions so that we learn the discipline of self-growth. However, this is not an easy win, it is a fight, but the glory of it is Jesus already won the war; we just have to believe in winning the battles that pop up in our lives for fine-tuning our faith in God.

Yes, the marathon is a life of integrity connected to understanding the Word as the power that ignites within the mind and spirit for empowering our hearts to courage, forcing the victory for self-work, and by faith transforming it to Spirit work of the soul. Meaning, we furnish the humility to embrace truth and agree with God regardless of the pain it may cause as we look at the good, bad and ugly of our psyche and emotional life. To walk, according to google dictionary definition of walking: means to move at a regular pace by lifting and setting down each foot in turn, never having both feet off the ground at once. So it is a journey. It is a rhythm of living and serving God through the revelation of the Word. The scripture teaches it is a pace, a skilled rhythm.

Ecclesiastes 9:11 KJV

[11] I returned, and saw under the sun, that the race is not to the swift, nor the battle to the strong, neither yet bread to the wise, nor yet riches to men of understanding, nor yet favour to men of skill; but time and chance happeneth to them all.

It is necessary to get in rhythm with the Spirit so that our spiritual timing is succinct with God's will. When we are in rhythm with God, we are poured into by the Holy Spirit. This is only possible as we learn to recognize God's presence, embrace God's Word and discern where we need to grow, hear, and obey God more efficiently. When a watch does not keep good time, chances are it needs a new battery. Well, God does not want to replace you but get you back in timing with Him so that you can keep time with the work of God toward the spectators that are sent of God to see your victory in Christ. We are the reflection of God's work in the earth made visible to those we encounter by His Spirit and is made visible to the natural eye through our transformation in the face of the world. A well-functioning watch helps the person wearing it be where they need to be on time and thereby enabling them to meet the demands of what that space and time were to accomplish. So it is in the Spirit when we walk in unity with Him, yielded to His adjustments to stay in rhythm with Him.

We find rhythm in the Spirit of God as we learn to not be held captive by our emotional life, dethroning all unhealthy emotions and thinking that throw you off from walking in the precision of timing with God. This is absolutely necessary to your actualization in God. Choosing which God you are going to serve, you as God or God the Father, is essential to the next steps for walking in the Spirit. Balancing unto change unhealthy emotional impulses is one of the attributes of spiritual maturity. Finding precision with God is spiritual. It is direct intentionality toward God that signifies He is first in your life. Doing the life-work to get in the flow of the Spirit is God's call to finishing the work He begins in you and produces fruit to His glory.

Learning to love God most, meaning with all your heart, is a necessary focus for being able to abide in the Spirit. This is an inner commitment of the heart, and we walk it out every day. Walking in the Spirit is a commitment to a relationship with God and not holding back anything from Him. However, this is a process and is not achieved overnight. We practice obedience and learn to sell out to God each day as we take up our cross daily and follow Him.

Luke 9:23 KJV

23 And he said to them all, if any man will come after me, let him deny himself, and take up his cross daily, and follow me.

God reveals Himself to you and reveals you to you as you walk with Him in the normal flow of your life. Even those truthful thorns provoke growth and change so that you can be more in sync with Him. Go on the inside of your heart and allow God's fellowship within you to impart and teach you about spiritual matters. This lifestyle becomes natural to your life rhythm; though it is spiritual, it is tangible, and as you learn to feel God and discern God's presence, you are enabled to hear more clearly. Hearing more clearly should provoke an intensity within to discern His will in response to feeling His presence.

Walking with God in the Spirit is provocative. It will pull you into closer accountability to God to please Him. Because He is the Spirit of Truth, anything that is contrary to truth challenge your rhythm with the Spirit. This call to more is to embrace the need to pursue characteristics that are like God. This happens as we apply the teachings of the Bible for taking on the nature of Christ. Walking with God for total transformation is a part pleasing God more fully. All of this is a choice. It is a spiritual conversion of the soul, spirit, and mind by which we are empowered by the Spirit of God that lives within.

Sensitivity to the Spirit of God demands time with Him, honesty about self, and intentionality to follow Him. This means attentiveness to hear, following, and obeying what the Holy Spirit says, whether in scripture, the routine of your life, or the things of ministry. It's not deep, but it is absolutely real. The Holy Spirit teaches us in response to an openness to learning. To strengthen your hearing means sacrificing some of your activities and time to get quiet in intentional devotions.

Devotions lead into the spiritual realm and cause sensitivity to the presence and move of God. They are passage into His presence. It is a precursor to Walking in the Spirit.

Disciplining one's self to set a date with God on a routine is your move toward unity with the Spirit. I can tell you from experience if you don't do this, you will not fully experience walking in the Spirit. So, decide to yield to the Holy Spirit, partner this mindset, and tie it all up with quality time spent in devotions for setting your environment for visitation from the Holy Spirit and then just yield, learn and obey. He is waiting on your passion to know Him and to be used by Him for His glory and your reward of blessing. Walking in the Spirit leads to an illumination of our entire life experience that nothing else can compete with.

Chapter 10: Illuminated by Walking in the Spirit

Some people can hardly believe the possibilities in Christ when we walk in the Spirit. We work so hard in trying to get things accomplished, not really grasping that when we truly yield to the Spirit of God and begin walking in Him, we find peace, joy, and achieve more than we ever imagined. Our human nature wants to achieve and accomplish, and in our culture, we are reared to believe it is in our education, knowledge, or skill sets. However, we are limited by our humanity and inability to control every variable. It takes God's influence in our lives to balance our lives and the events that hinder what we are trying to achieve. He graces what we put our hands to so that we are able to succeed according to His will. He seeds what we do to His glory and causes it to bring forth in our lives. It is the illumination of the Holy Spirit working

His wonder for our greatest outcomes.

Yes, the foundation for natural and spiritual success is accentuated beyond what we could ever do on our own when we walk with God in the Spirit. Walking with God positions us to be successful in all things as we have an authentic relationship with Him. Not only this, but when we please the Lord, He will give us that deep down unspoken desire of the heart. As we engage others, they will see the light of God's imprint on our lives and in our character, causing others to be attracted to Him.

This revelation of your relationship with God will cause others who do not know God to see the reflection of God in you as well as the difference that it makes in your life. What I am saying is that when you are able to survive and thrive in situations that you would not have survived, they know it is because of something more than what comes naturally to us, and so they become inquisitive. I remember years ago when I was in the workplace, and people would say, how did you get through that or who told you to do that, how did you know.

In 1989, I lived in Oakland, California, during the **The Loma Prieta earthquake** that caused 63 deaths, 3,757 injuries[2], and about $6 billion in damage. I lived a stone's throw away. At that time, I worked in San Francisco, California, for Blue Cross Insurance. I was at work, and the Spirit of God told me to leave and go home. I called my boss and told her I needed to go home, and she questioned me. I was reluctant to say God told me to leave and go home. I did not feel like telling her why, so she released me as she was out of state. I called my husband, who was at work and asked him to pick me up as God had told me to go home. He came and picked me up. We drove unto the Bay Bridge, and as soon as we crossed the end of the bridge unto the road in Oakland, we felt the car shaking, and my husband said,

---

[2] National Geographic Society. (2014, September 04). Loma Prieta Earthquake. Retrieved from https://www.nationalgeographic.org/thisday/oct17/loma-prieta-earthquake/

I think we have a flat tire. Then all of a sudden, the car rocked and reeled, and we saw the dust shoot up in the air looked like about 1000 feet, and we heard the sound of the freeway collapsing that we had just exited, followed by screaming and sirens, etc.

I immediately understood in the Spirit that the city was in trouble, and God had protected us and sent us across the bridge and held the earthquake until we could get across the bridge to our kids. All other staff at my office either had to stay at the office overnight or at a friend's place in the city as all modes of transportation from San Francisco to Oakland were immediately shut down. It was horrifying, but I was on fire with worship as it was crystal clear to my husband and me that God had protected our children and us when He told me to get up now and go home.

Well, it is obvious when others were trapped, and I was the only one in the entire building who lived across the bridge that made it home. The whole office was talking about it as my boss said Sharon asked me to go home and told me it was urgent that she leave right now to get home and across the bridge. They were all trapped for about 4-5 days before they were able to get out of the city to get home, but I had made it because of walking in the Spirit. I could hear God and had learned His voice and he had taught me to obey when He spoke to me. This event was the talk of the office, and when she called three days later and asked how did you know to leave, I was able to tell her and my office about my relationship with God and that God had told me. She was astonished and told the entire office about it. To God Be the

Glory for the things He has done and has used me to do. From that experience, I was asked at company events to pray over the food, etc. When we walk in the Spirit, and the light of His presence illuminates your life, others will see Him in you, and as you learn to obey, the Spirit of God will use you the way He wants, this is walking in the Spirit when we yield and obey. I tell you, the illumination of the Holy Spirit on fire inside of me caused me to be hot with evangelism. He taught me how to move in the Spirit through these types of events. The earthquakes were one of several revelations of the Spirit of God living in me to others.

Boy, the power of His presence and anointing is intoxicating and if you can be addicted to anything, let it be God's Spirit. It is the drink of a lifetime. One that only empowers and is able to be felt by others because He is just that real! These were opportunities for me to introduce God's presence and power in the life of an unbeliever. This illumination revelation is one of the ways how the Spirit of God witness to others through us. Our yielding to the work of the Holy Spirit within leads to a life of sharing God with others. He reveals His presence through our anointing, His light shining through, or an event where He manifests His protection or power in us.

I think I should, at this point, define my meaning of Illumination: 1. The act of physically **illuminating** or the condition of being filled with **light**: **light**, lighting. 2. Electromagnetic radiation that makes vision possible:

understanding illumination[3]. When we come to the Lord and become one with Him, we are illuminated by His presence, and the anointing will be not only powerful but will draw others to Him. It is impossible to be in God's presence and not be transformed by it. Why? Because He is light, truth, love, and power. When you spend time with Him routinely, you will be changed by His light. Light reveals anything contrary to it, so His light will provoke growth and spiritual maturity and challenge each of us to do better and to produce spiritual fruit for others to eat and be spiritually nourished.

I will never forget when I was first illuminated by the Spirit of God when I experienced His presence so strong that I felt I had entered another world, and I had. My initial encounter was salvation and then illumination of the Holy Spirit. It fills the soul and spirit for an epiphany that God is real, all-powerful, all-knowing, and wants a relationship with us. Since the initial baptism of the Holy Spirit, I have experienced refills as they are necessary. It is important to continue to seek out more and to stay on fire in God. But that first illumination of the Baptism of the Holy Spirit was most powerful, and nothing, I mean nothing, compares to it. It is love on steroids, empowerment, power, and God's presence. I was so drunk in the Spirit that I could not stand on my feet. I was drunk in the Spirit like the writings of Acts when the people thought they had drunk wine. This experience was the wine of the Holy Ghost, the illumination and indwelling Spirit of God, satiating the believer

---

[3] Illumination. (n.d.). Retrieved from https://www.thefreedictionary.com/illumination

with power to witness.

Acts 1:8-9 NKJV

[8] But you shall receive power when the Holy Spirit has come upon you; and you shall be [a] witnesses to Me in Jerusalem, and in all Judea and Samaria, and to the end of the earth."

This fulfillment of the promise of God to those who believe not only happened in the time of Acts but is still occurring in those who believe. It happened to me, I know that it is not only true but real. God wants to feel you if He hasn't already. Being filled with the Holy Spirit is so essential to your life and ability to walk in the Spirit. See, walking in the Spirit requires being filled with the Holy Spirit. You can't walk in what you do not have. The scripture tells us He is willing to give it to you if you ask.

Luke 11:12-14 KJV

[12] Or if he shall ask for an egg, will he offer him a scorpion? [13] If ye then, being evil, know how to give good gifts unto your children, how much more shall your heavenly Father give the Holy Spirit to them that ask Him?"

When we are illuminated by the Spirit, we affect our environment because we are influential in the Spirit. He is the X-factor that centers our lives, our relationships, and our ministry. This is why we must lean into Him and realize it is necessary for sustaining a victorious life as well as an impactful ministry. We lack the ability to fully fulfil God's will unless we are connected to the vine. He is indeed the source and resource that seeds our life success. An illuminated life is a life that is fueled by God's ever-present empowerment. This relationship with God is necessary to walking in the Spirit and reaping the harvest of spiritual provision, and God's fulfilled will. The abundant life Christ made possible for those who dare to live a life empowered and sold out to God will find their best life in walking in the Spirit.

Made in the USA
Middletown, DE
30 December 2021